Women Who Would Vote

The Dramatic Story
of the Daring Leaders
of the
Woman Suffrage
Movement

Jack Dempsey

Center for Creative Expression
Kitty Hawk, NC
2000

ISBN Number 1-57087-554-5

Library of Congress Catalog Card Number 00-135734

Center for Creative Expression
P.O. Box 210
Kitty Hawk, NC 27949
jujaka@aol.com

Manufactured in the United States of America
00 01 02 03 04   10 9 8 7 6 5 4 3 2 1

Preface

I was beginning to question my own judgment. I thought I had discovered a world war that lasted longer than World War I, World War II and the Cold War combined; was fought on more fronts than any shooting war; involved more combatants than any other war; started in the U.S. and spread to the entire developed world; and *almost no one seemed to know about it!* Could that be?

The latest film by Ken Burns and Paul Barnes on PBS in the fall of 1999 bolstered my confidence. *Not for Ourselves Alone* was their biography of Elizabeth Cady Stanton and Susan B. Anthony, 19th century suffragettes and women's rights leaders. Although the film itself was fascinating, what astounded me was the commentary on it at the end by Burns and Barnes.

They had just finished shooting their acclaimed documentary on the Civil War and were absorbed with the two-year chore of editing it. One morning, Barnes found a newspaper book review of a biography of Elizabeth Cady Stanton. It sounded interesting and, after further investigation, he concluded that Stanton had been one of the most influential persons, male or female, in the entirety of American history, *and he had never even heard of her.*

When Barnes shared with Ken Burns his astonishing finding, Burns admitted that he had never heard of Stanton, either. More than that, he expressed outrage that she and other leaders in her cause had been "written out of American history." Absolutely incredible! Together, Burns and Barnes decided to rectify the problem, at least in part. *Not for Ourselves Alone* became their means to that end.

Their story is part of a broader story that has appealed to me to the degree I feel compelled to tell it. Although there is no single starting point for the story, an argument can be made for the signing of the Declaration of Independence. That revered document set forth lofty ideals of equality for everyone and representation of everyone in the processes of society.

It was a wonderful message that gained the admiration of the world. Yet, over half of our nation's people remained without equality or representation. Slaves were the most obvious exception and all history books include extensive coverage of the later emancipation and enfranchisement (males only) of African-American slaves.

Between the extremes of slavery and equality, however, there was a middle status of oppression for which, incredibly, no one has coined a name. It was a status of totally restricted living. Tradition, customs, civil law and church dogma all ascribed the control of one-half of the population to the other half. Maledom controlled femaledom in every dimension of living. Although not slaves at one extreme, females lacked the promised equality and representation of males at the other. It was almost a caste system. Arguably, that's *exactly* what it was.

For seventy-two years after the Declaration of Independence, a few disgruntled women – very few – did complain about their lot in life, but none had the fortitude or capital or raw nerve to start a reform movement. Not until 1848. In that year in tiny Seneca Falls in upstate New York, Lucretia Mott and Elizabeth Stanton fired the shout heard 'round the world. Their women's rights convention, the first of its kind on planet Earth, jump-started a woman's rights movement that continues to this day.

Of all the goals considered by the participants at Seneca Falls, only woman suffrage was nearly defeated. Asking for the vote was considered too radical. Yet Stanton pushed it through and, over the ensuing decades, suffrage gradually grew to dominate the women's rights agenda. Every fiber in the cloth of society worked against the suffrage goal from the giddy beginning to the "bloody" end.

Other countries throughout the world were jolted out of complacency by the Seneca Falls Women's Rights Convention and began similar movements of their own. To their credit and our shame, over a dozen major countries throughout the world enfranchised their women before we did. Universal woman suffrage was not attained until 1920, a full 144 years after the Declaration of Independence introduced democracy to the world. Still, woman suffrage was, indeed, the first world war and it started here.

It *was* a war because feminist leaders had to fight tooth and nail for every inch of progress. They experienced ridicule in the press, defeat in the courts, derision in the legislatures, obstinacy at home and condemnation from the pulpits. They had to *fight* to win and that is my story.

Like Burns and Barnes, I stumbled across my story by sheer accident. It began in my childhood with the hobby of stamp collecting. Unlike those who looked for watermarks and counted perforations, I was interested in the stories behind the stamps. Who were all those people on the nation's envelopes and what were all those places and events? My frequent trips to the library to find out developed a lifelong fascination with history, especially American history.

College, graduate school, marriage and child rearing moved stamp collecting to the back burner for decades, even though I remained a history buff. Several years ago, however, a friend convinced me to join a new stamp club in the community. I did and I decided to revive my childhood hobby with a systematic study of the U.S. postal issues commemorating health professionals.

Health administration had been my career and I immediately recognized a stamp honoring Dr. Virginia Apgar, who had studied in the same Johns Hopkins department in which I earned my doctorate. Perhaps that sensitized me to gender, because I gradually became aware that few women had been commemorated in a field that traditionally has employed more females than others. Curiosity aroused, I began compiling a complete list of commemorated females in U.S. postal history, which was nearly one hundred at that time.

Then I aggregated like with like – writers, artists, entertainers, native Americans – and began reading short biographies one set at a time. I was particularly intrigued with early female aviators who had to fight for the right to fly in their day.

Then I discovered the suffragettes, the nineteenth and early twentieth century leaders who won suffrage for society's better half. Their lives absolutely fascinated me. How had my half-century of reading American history missed these people and their heroic struggle to emancipate themselves from a male-dominated caste system? Some place or other I had read about parades by women to get the vote, which they got and that was about it. If there had been more to it than that, the history books would have included it, wouldn't they?

After I had read everything I could buy from the local bookstores, I began ordering out-of-print and specialty books through my local library, which provided another surprise. Not a single book from a public or university library had averaged one checkout a year over the previous decade. In fact, several had not been checked out even once in the entire previous decade. Indeed, all the books were in the type of perfect condition that results from . . . *storage!*

Why is it that one half of the population has such little interest in the roots of its own emancipation?

I've written my story just as I discovered it, from the biographies of leaders. Actually, major leaders. Nearly all of the nineteenth and early twentieth century distinguished women whom the Postal Service had commemorated were associated with the woman suffrage movement to some degree. But I found that I could trace the entire movement through the lives of eight principal leaders, but no fewer. Commemorated persons such as Mary Lyon, Frances Willard and Clara Barton had supported suffrage, but were commemorated primarily for their contributions to other causes such as education (Lyon), temperance (Willard) and disaster services (Barton, founder of the American Red Cross). But I found the lives of eight women fully documented the two-generation woman suffrage movement.

Burns and Barnes produced a film on just part of the woman suffrage movement and it still consumed two TV evenings to show. The duration of the movement, the millions of participants and the dozens of related historical issues make a detailed story of the movement virtually impossible. The most serious attempt to do it was by a series of editors in the *History of Woman Suffrage* – a six-volume, 5,000 page monster-of-a-work. Most other authors, in an attempt to keep their work to conventional book length, focus only on part of the movement. Biographies of individual suffragettes are common.

My intention is to offer something unique. I want to tell the *whole* story of the movement from beginning to end. But I also want to tell it *succinctly* so that readers can grasp the whole story in a half-day's reading. Confining my narrative to eight *sine qua non* leaders makes that possible. Books with details on this or that dimension are readily available for additional reading, and I earnestly hope the reader continues.

Consequently, my book is for the beginner. I hope students of history, sociology, religion, government, race relations, women's studies, politics, leadership, social justice and countless other subjects will find my story revealing, captivating and an insight into the roots of democracy in our country. It is ideal for classes, courses, study groups and discussion groups of all types. It offers role models for young women and cause for reflection for men of all ages.

It is time this story receives the grateful attention it has long deserved and has not yet received from the general public.

Jack Dempsey

Contents

Preface   iii-viii

Chapter 1 - The First Step In the March
    of a Thousand Miles   1-10

Chapter 2 - The First Convention of Its
    Type in World History   11-22

Chapter 3 - Leadership Grows Before
    the Civil War   23-40

Chapter 4 - 1860-1870: War, Conflict,
    Defeat and Division   41-52

Chapter 5 - Gridlock: 1870-1899 -- The
    Context   53-66

Chapter 6 - Gridlock: 1870-1899 -- Inch
    By Inch Progress   67-90

Chapter 7 - The Agony and the Ecstasy   91-109

Appendix I - State-by-State Progress in Full
    and Presidential Woman Suffrage   110

Appendix II - The 1848 Seneca Falls
    Women's Rights Convention   111-115

Guide to Further Reading   116-119

Chapter 1

The First Step In the March of

a Thousand Miles

It was August 26, 1920. Young Harry Burns sat in Tennessee's legislature with the fate of millions of American women in his hands. Thirty-five other states had previously voted for ratification of the Nineteenth Amendment to the Constitution for enfranchising women -- one short of the necessary number -- and Burns held the deciding vote for Tennessee. Pondering his decision, he recalled his mother's command to be a "good boy" and "help Mrs. Catt put the 'Rat' in Ratification" (Hymowitz, p. 284). Although history has not recorded what agonizing punishment Mrs. Burns had in store for young Harry if he disobeyed her, he clearly wished to avoid the misery and voted YES to ratification.

Woman suffrage had become the law of the land! In one monumentally emotional moment, Burns ended a 72-year struggle by women's organizations to win access to the ballot box. The most elusive, most resisted goal of the women's rights movement had been finally -- oh, finally! -- realized.

The goal of woman suffrage had been formulated formally for the first time in an upstate New York women's rights convention in 1848. After it, the cause consumed the lives of two generations of leaders to bring the dream into reality. Mrs. Carrie Catt, to whom Harry Burn's mother referred, led the final charge to victory.

Although women in contemporary society are still striving for complete equality, it is difficult to exaggerate how much progress has been made and especially how right-less women were at the beginning of the struggle. Married women "back then" were little more than household possessions of their husbands. All women were expected to be silent in public and no reputable woman would travel alone. The wages of working women were paid to their husbands or fathers. No college accepted them. As in many of today's organizations, they received less pay than males for the same work (e.g., teachers), but *much* less then. And they could not vote in national, state and most local elections.

That such conditions still persist in many countries of the world makes those unthinkable conditions somewhat understandable. And a brief review of our country's early history also makes understandable why the United States was an early leader in redressing the grievances of the female gender, incomplete though the process still remains. Without our unique early history, a climate for women leaders would not have been possible, and women leaders were absolutely essential. No benevolent, male-dominated society in history had graciously granted rights to women, especially not suffrage. Winning rights took muscle and sweat and perseverance and vision and great personal risks, and women leaders did all of that. The American woman's struggle for suffrage and other rights is absolutely awesome and deserves the rapt attention of all who might otherwise forget . . . .

A Context for Leadership

The idea of emigrating to the New World held little appeal for most English citizens. Sir Walter Raleigh's first attempt at colonization in North Carolina resulted in the Lost Colony. Hostile Spanish ships patrolled the coast. The Jamestown settlers learned why native "savages" were so named. Early settlers found no gold or other get-rich-quick opportunities. All in all, a harsh life could be expected. It's not surprising, therefore, that many of the first settlers were more highly motivated to leave England and other European countries than they were to move to the New World. What they lacked there was tolerance of their religious beliefs; what they sought here was religious *freedom.*

Schoolchildren routinely learn about the Pilgrims and Puritans in New England, the Quakers and Mennonites in Pennsylvania, the Catholics in Maryland and all manner of sects throughout the colonies -- all seeking religious freedom in the New World. Although most of the arriving denominations extended as much tolerance to other denominations as they wanted for themselves, occasional intolerance evoked responses quite revealing of the emerging values of the times.

In one such instance in 1658, Peter Stuyvesant, a Dutch West Indies Company governor in New Amsterdam (later New York), issued a restrictive edict concerning newly arriving Quaker immigrants. Citizens in Flushing resented the edict and remonstrated as follows (excerpts from the *Flushing Remonstrance*):

Right Honorable. You have been pleased to send up unto us a certain Prohibition or Command, that wee shoulde not receive or entertain any of

3

those people called Quakers, because they are
supposed to bee by some seducers of the people;
for our parte wee cannot condemn them in this
case . . . our desire is not to offend any one of
(God's) little ones in whatsoever forme, name or
title hee appears in, whether Presbyterian,
Independent, Baptist or Quaker, but shall be
glad to see anything of God in any of them:
desireing to doe unto all men as wee desire all
men should doe unto us, which is the true law
both of Church and State.

Implicit in this message is *equality* among men in the
eyes of God *and* of the state. Thus it is a short jump from
religious freedom and equality to civil freedom and
equality, which was precisely what was written into the
1776 Declaration of Independence:

We hold these truths to be self-evident, that all
men are created equal, that they are endowed by
their Creator with certain unalienable Rights,
that among these are Life, Liberty and the
pursuit of Happiness. That to secure these rights,
Governments are instituted among Men, deriving
their just powers from the consent of the
governed.

It was, indeed, a revolutionary message. Gone were
unearned privileges for the few. Power was now vested in
individuals at the bottom, not at the top, of the institutional
hierarchy and government was charged with protecting that
power as a right.

The rights in the Declaration and in the first ten
amendments to the new Constitution (Bill of Rights) were
recognized by all thirteen colonies. They constituted the

4

nucleus of a national code of values against which the status of society could be measured. The revolting colonials had not only won the war, but had secured an entirely new way of viewing and protecting the individuals in society.

Not all aspects of post-revolutionary society fared well in the light of the new values. Most especially, how could one believe all men were created equal and also own slaves?

Abolition, then, became the first reform goal among those who found social practices incompatible with our founding principles. The abolition movement also brought together reform-minded individuals who organized, petitioned, agitated and engaged in any and all activities to further the cause. *And it provided a training ground for leaders who would later expand their reform energies to encompass other causes . . . such as women's rights.*

This was the context, then, from which woman suffrage leaders emerged. There was an accepted code of social values, a Constitution with explicit human rights, a clear violation of those rights and a training ground in reform organizations. Enter the first female leader.

Lucretia Mott (1793-1880)

It takes many adjectives even to begin describing Lucretia Mott. Dedicated, tireless, a caring wife and mother, determined, creative, persuasive, aggressive, articulate, daring. More than anything, however, *religious.*

Lucretia Coffin had the good fortune to be reared in a Quaker family. More formally known as the Society of Friends, the Quaker religion frowned on any type of hierarchy, privilege or rank. Everyone was equal in the eyes of God -- a sentiment in complete consonance with the

Declaration of Independence's "all men are created equal" theme. This included Quaker women even to the degree of becoming ministers. Lucretia spoke openly in religious services, something not tolerated in the wider society, and was accepted as a Quaker minister before the age of 30.

This acceptance contrasted sharply with the fate of others in earlier times and in a different climate of values. In the 1630s, Anne Hutchinson, the daughter of a Puritan minister, defied custom in Boston by speaking liberally on religious matters. Branded a heretic by Puritan leaders, she and her family were banished, later being massacred by Indians on Long Island. Mary Dyer, a Quaker convert and almost alone in her outspoken defense of Hutchinson, defied Massachusetts' law banning Quakers, visiting Boston frequently to preach. On June 1, 1660, the Puritan theocracy *hanged* her.

Lucretia did more than just talk in Quaker meetings. She extended her ministerial vision to the active pursuit of social reform. With lifelong support from her husband, she devoted much of her youthful energy to the abolition movement. From her Philadelphia home, she led a boycott of goods produced by slave labor. She and her husband harbored runaway slaves in direct violation of the law. She repeatedly spoke against slavery in public when women just *didn't* speak in public. She joined, supported and founded abolition organizations. All of these she did in the context of her ministerial mission and at a time when women were expected to content themselves with knitting.

It was not surprising, therefore, that Lucretia was appointed a delegate to the World Anti-Slavery Convention in London in 1840. Influential persons in many countries were re-examining their positions on slavery at that time, making the 1840 convocation the first major international one of its kind. Few in the United States had earned a greater right to go than Lucretia. She gladly accepted the responsibility, totally unaware of the brouhaha that awaited her and its relevance to women's rights.

It's not entirely clear what experiences before the London convention had molded Lucretia's opinions on the inequality of women in society. Certainly her upbringing had been one. Born into a sea captain's family on Nantucket Island, young Lucretia saw her mother run the family business during her father's long absences at sea. And her father's insistence on "educating his daughters to usefulness" was atypical of the times.

Certainly her first work experience opened her eyes. When she completed her education in mid-adolescence and began to teach, she found that, although a female's education cost the same as a male's, the female teacher earned less than half of a male's income after graduation.

Additionally, Lucretia was more than a little fortunate to marry fellow Quaker, James Mott, who supported her "unconventional" pursuits throughout their lifetime in Philadelphia.

And certainly the principles of her religion, which she embraced without question, predisposed her to the notion of equal rights for women, a foreign notion to most of her contemporaries.

It is not known how much the writings of Mary Wollstonecraft influenced Mott. That English woman's *A Vindication of the Rights of Woman* in 1792 became a Bible for many nineteenth century American feminists. Wollstonecraft was also the first woman to observe in writing how the values in the Declaration of Independence invited a movement toward equality of woman.

It also is not known whether Jacksonian democracy in the 1830s sharpened her vision of woman suffrage, if at all. In Jackson's time, not even all the white males had the vote. In most areas, land-owning white males controlled the ballot box, and sometimes only Protestant ones. Jackson argued forcefully before and during his presidency for expanding male suffrage. It's a short, logical step to extend it to females, but it's not clear whether Mott drew that conclusion from Jackson's premises.

It's not even clear whether Lucretia's enormous time commitment to religion, family, abolition and temperance left any time for women's rights beyond thinking about them. But the 1840 debacle at London's World Anti-Slavery Convention brought her thoughts into sharp relief. It was then and there that world-class liberals, convened to condemn the despicable practice of slavery, denied convention admittance to Mott and other Americans *because they were women.* Liberals!

Accustomed to rude, occasionally rough, treatment in her abolition work, Lucretia kept her cool head, but unleashed her tongue. Some male members of the convention called her a "spitfire" and some local newspapers dubbed her the "lioness of the convention." She gave an impromptu, uninvited, poorly received speech at a breakfast meeting, and she argued her position forcefully at credential committees.

Mott's occupation of the moral high ground and her impeccable logic left male conventioneers frustrated and angry. One entry in her diary reveals her perception of the effect she had on some of the men. And it reveals that male chauvinism included some delegates from the United States such as Rev. Nathaniel Colver, pastor of the First Free Baptist Church in Boston.

Prescod of Jamaica (colored) thought it would lower the dignity of the Convention and bring ridicule on the whole thing if ladies were admitted -- he was told similar reasons were urged in Philadelphia for the exclusion of colored people from our meetings -- but had we yielded on such flimsy argument, we might as well have abandoned our enterprise. Colver thought Women constitutionally unfit for public or business meetings -- he was told that the colored man too was said to be constitutionally unfit to mingle with the white man. He left the room angry.

All to no avail. Women were not accepted. The battle was lost.

The battle was lost . . . *fortunately*. During the time *not* spent at convention proceedings, middle-aged Lucretia Mott from Pennsylvania forged a lasting relationship with a young honeymooning woman from upstate New York -- Elizabeth Cady Stanton.

The older, wiser and more experienced woman articulated her vision of a world with equality for women. The younger woman eagerly absorbed every word, astonished and exhilarated by her new friend's dream. They discussed the possibility of founding a women's rights movement patterned on the organized abolition movement when they returned to the States. If the narrow-mindedness of the liberal men in London were any indication at all, it clearly would be an uphill fight all the way.

However, the woman's rights movement finally had its first two leaders-in-waiting:
Lucretia Coffin Mott (1793-1880)
Elizabeth Cady Stanton (1815-1902)

Chapter Appendix

The Quaker Women

One marvels at the omnipresence of Quaker women in the suffrage movement, both those reared in that denomination and those influenced by it. Lucretia Mott, Susan B. Anthony and Alice Paul came from Quaker families. Runaway slave, Sojourner Truth, was harbored by Quakers and both lived and worshipped with them during her adjustment to emancipated living. Elizabeth Stanton shunned formal denominational affiliation in her adult years, but drew support from Quaker beliefs and supportive relationships with a few ministers. Thus, of the eight principal suffrage leaders discussed here, only Lucy Stone, Julia Ward Howe and Carrie Catt found inspiration elsewhere.

The Grimke sisters also found safe harbor in the Quaker denomination and contributed to the Quaker movement in an indirect, unusual way before the movement even began. Angelina and Sarah were born and raised on a southern plantation with slaves. Sickened by the practice of slavery that they saw, they left their home and their Episcopal denomination, becoming abolition Quakers in the North. Although the taboo against women speaking in public was still present in the 1830s, they found themselves in demand throughout the North to describe before audiences the evils they had personally witnessed in southern plantations. Thus, they successfully violated the taboo because they had a message people wanted to hear, thereby easing the way for later feminists with a subject people *didn't* want to hear.

One wonders how the suffrage movement would have fared without Quaker women.

Chapter 2

The First Convention of Its Type

In World History

Away-from-home convention resolutions usually fare no better than New Year's resolutions. Such was the case with Lucretia Coffin Mott and Elizabeth Cady Stanton upon their return from the London-based World Anti-Slavery Convention in 1840. Mott was swept along by the burgeoning abolition movement and newly married Stanton experienced the first of her seven pregnancies.

But there was a difference. Mott's diary of the London convention contained frequent reference to her enjoyable encounters with Stanton, but nothing about a new women's rights movement. Instead, her first love, the abolition movement, dominated her writings.

In Stanton's diary, by contrast, Mott and women's rights commanded center stage. Even a continuous series of pregnancies could not extinguish her new vision of the lot of women in life.

Elizabeth Cady's developmental years north of Albany, NY had differed markedly from Mott's. Her father, a conservative Presbyterian and a lawyer, followed the times' double standard in child rearing. When his son died and Elizabeth tried to take his place, he benevolently informed her she couldn't because she was just a girl. More than that, Elizabeth saw a steady stream of depressed, tearful women leaving her father's law office; upon inquiry, she learned that women, especially married women, enjoyed virtually no protection under the law.

At the same time, her academic excellence earned her an advanced placement with a dozen boys in an honors class. When the boys graduated and left for college at its conclusion, Elizabeth sat at home because not a single U.S. college accepted females at that time.

Even so, her relatively late marriage to Henry Stanton in her mid-twenties followed many enjoyable years as a single woman. She was a skilled horsewoman who also enjoyed skating, sledding and outdoor life in general. She was an extrovert's extrovert, relishing all manner of social engagements. Family and friends filled her days.

She even busied herself with the local abolition group, where she met Henry Stanton, a liberal journalist and soon-to-be lawyer. Against her father's advice, she married Stanton and asserted her individuality at the outset: the marriage vows were stripped of any mention of "obey."

Soon after their London honeymoon, the Stantons moved to Boston. The stimulating cultural environment there provided welcome relief from the constant demands of an ever-growing brood of children.

In 1847, the bubble burst. Henry moved his fledgling law practice to tiny Seneca Falls in northwestern New York, not far from the Canadian border. Outgoing Elizabeth, separated from friends, family and a rich cultural environment, entered a state of depression. Her letters revealed a deep dissatisfaction with the new state of affairs.

In 1848, all that changed for the rest of her life. Lucretia and James Mott visited friends in the area and, of course, dropped by to visit Elizabeth. The eight-year separation since the London convention evaporated almost instantly. They and a few of Stanton's friends decided to hold a women's rights convention. Immediately. Right there in tiny, remote, unsophisticated Seneca Falls.

The Seneca Falls
Woman's Rights Convention

The short, July 14 announcement in The Seneca County Courier, a semi-weekly newspaper, came right to the point.

A convention to discuss the social, civil and religious condition and rights of woman, will be held in the Wesleyan Chapel, at Seneca Falls, N.Y., on Wednesday and Thursday, the 19th and 20th of July, current; commencing at 10 o'clock, A.M.

A surprising 300 persons, mostly women, were attracted to the outrageously daring convention in spite of the short notice to a small town and rural population in a limited circulation newspaper. It undoubtedly sounded like something new, lively and exciting.

Lucretia Mott made the opening and closing comments and James Mott chaired the proceedings. But Elizabeth Stanton's Declaration of Sentiments became the cornerstone of the convention. Her prepared remarks were as confrontational as the Declaration of Independence because they followed its logical flow, frequently copying whole sections of it *verbatim*, except for occasional modifications (italics mine):

> We hold these truths to be self-evident: that all
> men *and women* are created equal; that they are
> endowed by their Creator with certain
> inalienable rights; . . . that to secure these rights
> governments are instituted, deriving their just
> powers from the consent of the governed . . . .
> Such has been the patient sufferance of the
> *women* under this government, and such is now
> the necessity which constrains them to demand
> the equal station to which they are entitled.

Stanton's text creates some confusion as to whether the culprit in question was government or *man*kind generally -- the two overlap but do have their differences. The section excerpted above incriminates government, but the list of over a dozen grievances sampled and excerpted below states "he" has established an "absolute tyranny" over "her."

The following grievances target employment, education and religion -- mostly non-governmental.

> He has monopolized nearly all the profitable
> employments, and from those she is permitted to
> follow, she receives but a scanty remuneration.

> He has denied her the facilities for obtaining a
> thorough education, all colleges being closed
> against her.

> He allows her in Church . . . but a subordinate
> position (excluding her) from any public
> participation in the affairs of the Church.

Yet, most of the grievances involve male-dominated government -- exclusively or in part. In this Stanton differentiates between married and single women. When legal traditions developed in the Old World, female children were covered by their fathers' rights and they remained at home until they married, thereafter covered by their husbands' rights. Even today, the father "gives" the bride to the groom, like a baton in a relay. The single woman, by contrast, had rights of her own because legal tradition simply had not foreseen her existence. That is, she had rights by default.

In this context, Elizabeth Stanton protested that rightless married women could not sue in court, own property, form an egalitarian marital relationship or get a fair shake in divorce. The single woman fared better, but only marginally.

> **He has made her, if married, in the eye of the law, civilly dead.**
>
> **He has taken from her all right in property, even to the wages she earns.**
>
> **. . . in the covenant of marriage, she is compelled to promise obedience to her husband, he becoming, to all intents and purposes, her master . . . .**
>
> **. . . if single, and the owner of property, he has taxed her to support a government which recognizes her only when her property can be made profitable to it.**

Important as these and other grievances were to Stanton and the women in attendance, the position of honor at the beginning of the list went to Elizabeth's most cherished cause -- enfranchisement. Without the vote, how could women hold representatives accountable?

He has never permitted her to exercise her inalienable right to the elective franchise.

He has compelled her to submit to laws, in the formation of which she had no voice.

After these and other grievances, Stanton clearly warmed to the task of summarizing the grand totality of man's inhumanity to women. Jovial, kindly and caring by temperament, she also demonstrates here an admirable capacity for landing a smashing uppercut.

Now, in view of this entire disfranchisement of one-half of the people in this country, their social and religious degradation, -- in view of the unjust laws above mentioned, and because women do feel themselves aggrieved, oppressed, and fraudulently deprived of their most sacred rights, we insist that they have immediate admission to all the rights and privileges which belong to them as citizens of these United States.

Almost hidden in this flurry of punches is the expansion of the feminist argument for equality. To this point, the argument had rested on gaining God-given rights. Here Elizabeth added the rights of citizenship. Shortly after the Civil War, the rights of citizenship would become a crucial issue and would gradually dominate the feminist argument.

Following the Declaration of Grievances came a series of 12 resolutions to be voted on by those in attendance. Compared to the specific grievances, the resolutions seemed a surprisingly general repetition.

Resolved, That woman is man's equal -- was intended to be so by the Creator, and the highest

**good of the race demands that she should be
recognized as such.**

**Resolved, That inasmuch as man . . . does accord
to woman moral superiority, it is pre-eminently
his duty to encourage her to speak and teach . . .
in all religious assemblies.**

But the shortest of all the resolutions, getting the vote,
drew formidable fire from both men and women in
attendance.

**Resolved, That it is the duty of the women of this
country to secure to themselves their sacred
right to the elective franchise.**

Even those who considered the resolution admirable
argued that it was going too far. It was just asking for
trouble. It puts all the other, more reasonable resolutions in
jeopardy. Even Lucretia Mott waffled momentarily on this
resolution, but finally came to Stanton's aid by supporting
it.

An unexpected voice of support came from Frederick
Douglass, an African-American abolitionist with a national
reputation. He argued that gaining the vote was the first
step to securing many other rights.

Douglass was not the first abolitionist to support
women's rights. William Lloyd Garrison, a major U.S.
abolition leader, had refused his seat at the 1840 London
Anti-Slavery Convention because women were not
accepted. On the surface, at least, abolitionism and
women's rights were mutually supportive, at least until after
the Civil War of 1861-1865.

But why should woman suffrage have caused the
greatest furor at the convention? In contemporary America,

after all, it's not unusual for less than half of all registered voters to exercise their right. Political parties and special interest groups work diligently to "get out the vote," frequently failing.

Perhaps the answer lies in the fact that voting is no longer a special privilege. Nearly universal suffrage makes it a rather ordinary right that many take for granted. Such has been the case neither in world history nor in nineteenth century America. In most societies in which at least some things were put to the vote, restricting voting rights was a *control* mechanism. In various times and places, voting eligibility has been determined by citizenship, property ownership, length of residence, registration, religion, sex, age, poll tax payment, education, criminal record, absenteeism or class. In some instances, the "establishment" had been benevolently motivated to keep *control* in the hands of those deemed most likely to vote for the good of the community. In other instances, the establishment just wanted to stay in *control*.

Stanton and many of her contemporaries felt *controlled* by the male's monopoly of the ballot box, resented it deeply and made it a symbol of their lack of *control* over their persons, families and communities. After all, it was fresh in their minds that a *war* had recently been fought with England over, in part, lack of representation.

Most of those at the convention had not invested years analyzing the lot of women as Mott and Stanton had. They probably found the early proceedings quite entertaining. But asking for woman suffrage seemed a bit much. And it could make bigger waves than they cared to chance. So, even though they finally adopted the suffrage resolution, many had grave misgivings about adding their signatures to the list of resolutions.

As it turned out, they were right.

Almost over night, news of the unprecedented, preposterous proceedings at Seneca Falls reached the country's newspapers, with predictable results. The male dominated press attacked the very nature of the convention, ridiculed it and some even reproduced the proceedings so that all might see for themselves just how ludicrous the whole endeavor was. Back in Seneca Falls, some who had signed the resolutions sought to have their names removed. Considering that only 100 (68 women and 32 men) of the c. 300 attendees had signed in the first place, unanimity certainly had not characterized the convention.

But the newspapers miscalculated. Unintentionally, they gave Mott and Stanton and all their supporters more publicity than they ever could have afforded to buy. Here and there in countless homes across the country, disgruntled women and fair-minded men read about the Seneca Falls Woman's Rights Convention with great relief.

At last, some people were trying to do something! At last!

*   *   *

Stanton and especially Mott knew full well progress would be slow. Both had been rudely treated before in their abolition work. Still, the agenda for reform they helped forge at the convention is somewhat surprising.

> **We shall employ agents, circulate tracts, petition the State and National legislatures, and endeavor to enlist the pulpit and press on our behalf. We hope this Convention will be followed by a series of Conventions embracing every part of the country.**

Essentially this called for a public relations campaign to influence the public's attitude toward equal rights for women. Absent were twentieth century strategies of demonstrations, sit-ins, strikes, class action suits and Constitutional amendments.

Such an agenda required massive personpower, but Stanton was tied down with babies and Mott's abolition responsibilities were forbidding. They needed help drastically, but where would it come from? Fortunately, it was nearer than they imagined.

Chapter Appendix

The Softer Side

All the women's rights leaders were very strong persons who showed that side of themselves consistently every time they occupied the spotlight. Behind closed doors, however, they all had moments of doubt, emotional crises and discouragement. They were all hurt deeply from time to time when persons close to them rejected them, betrayed them or otherwise let them down. During those private times, those strong leaders felt anything but the heroes others were making of them. Their perseverance during such times is what set them apart.

There was one such private moment in the young life of Elizabeth Cady Stanton that was particularly poignant and revealing of the tender side of a reformer's life. It was 1854 and Elizabeth had been invited to address New York's legislature for the first time in her life. It was a monumental milestone. Her father read of it in the newspaper and wrote her to stop by to see him on her way to Albany. He wanted to hear her speech.

Elizabeth did so with trepidation. She had loved her lawyer-father deeply as a child but never received the approval she craved from him. Worse, he opposed her public life as a reformer. What type of hurt would he inflict on her on the eve of a major achievement in her life? She describes the experience in her autobiography (pp. 187-189):

> ... late one evening, when he was alone in his office, I entered and took my seat on the opposite side of his table. On no occasion, before or since, was I ever more embarrassed -- an audience of one, and that the one of all others whose approbation I most desired, whose disapproval I most feared. I knew he condemned the whole movement, and was deeply grieved at the active part I had taken.

Trembling, Elizabeth started reading her speech, describing in detail the humiliating circumstances of many of the state's women.

> ... to my intense satisfaction, I saw tears filling my father's eyes. I cannot express the exultation I felt, thinking that now he would see, with my eyes, the injustice women suffered under the laws he knew so well.

> (When she had finished, he) did not speak for a long time. ... At last, turning abruptly, he said: "Surely you have had a happy, comfortable life, with all your wants and needs supplied; and yet that speech fills me with self-reproach; for one might naturally ask, how can a young woman, tenderly brought up, who has had no bitter personal experience, feel so keenly the wrongs of her sex? Where did you learn this lesson?" "I learned it here," I replied, "in your

office, when a child, listening to the complaints women made to you."

How he felt on the question after that I do not know, as he never said anything in favor of or against it.

The term, inner directed, has been applied to those who draw strength from within because outside support and direction is lacking. The suffrage leaders, especially in the beginning, were truly inner directed because frequently they found themselves alone in storms of criticism and abuse.

Chapter 3

Leadership Grows Before the Civil War

Although the Declaration of Grievances at the 1848 Seneca Falls Woman's Rights Convention accurately portrayed the status of women in society, it did contain a major factual error. The statement that no college in the country accepted women ignored the founding of Oberlin College in Ohio more than a decade earlier. It accepted both blacks and women, the only college in the country to do so.

The statement also ignored the founding of Mount Holyoke Female Seminary in Massachusetts a decade before the Seneca Falls convention. It was founded *by* a woman *for* women.

Interestingly, one leader-to-be attended both.

Lucy Stone (1818-1893)

Lucy Stone was the eighth of nine children in a typical farm family in western Massachusetts -- typical in that her father, like Elizabeth Stanton's, envisioned only a domestic role for his female offspring. Her mother agonized over her hard life and Lucy agonized over her Congregationalist church's repressive Biblical interpretation of woman's place in society. She decided at a remarkably young age to seek a better lot in life than what was generally available to females at the time. Lucy's first goal was to stay in school longer than the minimum to become a teacher at age 16. Unlike Stanton's father, Lucy's considered that frivolous and made her sign an IOU for the expenses of her education. She did become a teacher and later, in her early 20s (1839), enrolled in Mount Holyoke Female Seminary -- a year-old, totally unique facility. She was quite fortunate to gain entrance because over 400 applicants for the school's second year were refused entrance for lack of space. Mothers and their daughters were simply frantic to find an academic environment different from a finishing school's.

Founded by visionary Mary Lyon in South Hadley, Massachusetts, Mount Holyoke substituted algebra for dance and French for Dishwashing 101. Eighty students of at least 17 years of age began their studies in 1837. The school lacked a four year curriculum at first and no one dared call it a college, but its standards rivaled any male college of the times.

Most innovative of all was the school's work-study program. Mary Lyon explicitly wanted an affordable education for academically talented young women, irrespective of whether their families were poor or unwilling to "waste" money on their daughters' education. It was well-suited to Stone's needs.

But it wasn't exactly what Lucy wanted, so she left in her first year. Instead, she set her sights on the new Oblerlin College in Ohio, which had opened a few years before Mount Holyoke. She saved enough money to enroll there at age 25, graduating with a B.A. in 1847, the year before the Seneca Falls convention. Thus, she became the first Massachusetts woman to earn a college degree, and was one of the first in the entire country.

Yet, even trail-blazing Oberlin College offered a mixed experience for Stone. The curriculum for women had a strong domestic quality to it and women were treated differently. They were required, for instance, to take debating classes, but were denied the right to actually debate. Lucy promptly organized some of her "fellow" students into groups which debated clandestinely off-campus.

Although Lucy Stone's commitment to women's rights had been evident since childhood, the Oberlin experience additionally and specifically committed her to the abolition cause. When the college opened, students transferred *en masse* from Cincinnati's Lane Theological Seminary, which had suppressed their abolitionist activities. Oberlin not only tolerated them, but also accepted some black students and became a station in the underground railroad. Lucy thoroughly internalized the values of the movement.

She also became convinced that her future career would lie in public speaking, a daring ambition considering society's still active taboo against women speaking in public. Given this aspiration, her time at Oberlin ended on a sour note. She was invited to write a graduation speech, but it had to be read by a man. Outraged, she refused, took her "bachelor" of arts degree and left in 1847.

Stone had come to the attention of abolition leader William Lloyd Garrison during her Oberlin days and actively sought employment from him as an anti-slavery public speaker. After her graduation and her first speech in 1847 at a church pastored by her brother, she accepted an offer to do just that for Garrison's Massachusetts-based

American Anti-Slavery Association. On weekends, she spoke on abolition; during the week, on women's rights.

Lucy quickly gained a reputation as a skilled orator, much in demand. At the time, the lecture circuit provided many males with a fine living because, without television or radio or an efficient postal system, it was an enlightening and entertaining way of hearing the news. Given the taboo against women speakers and the highly controversial topics of women's rights and abolition, Lucy's sex and topics guaranteed a perilous career. Crowds repeatedly jeered her, roughed her up on at least one occasion and even hosed her down during an outdoor, mid-winter speech.

Even Lucy's education landed her in trouble. When she objected to mis-translations of the Bible that demeaned women, her Congregationalist church excommunicated her.

It is not surprising, therefore, that she felt isolated in her cause. No one of significance openly supported her women's rights views except Garrison, whose controversial reputation made him a questionable ally. He argued for the immediate abolition of slavery, in conflict with those who advocated phasing it out. And his confrontational style alienated many of those who did agree with him, especially clergymen.

Whereas Lucretia Mott had the support of her husband and her Quaker church, and Elizabeth Stanton had the support of Mott and at least the tolerance, if not active support, of her husband, Stone stood alone!

All that changed in July of 1848. The Seneca Falls convention directed a beacon of hope to her. There were, after all, other people out there just like her, and *they were banding together.*

The Seneca Falls convention had called for more conventions, and Lucy Stone was one of the first to respond. With guidance from Lucretia Mott and others, she became the driving force behind the first national women's rights convention in Worcester Massachusetts, in 1850. Over 1,000 persons attended and the press, pro and con, covered every detail of the proceedings.

Interestingly, suffrage drew much less reaction than it had in Seneca Falls. And it continued to draw less fire in the nearly annual conventions Lucy backed prior to the Civil War. The 1850 convention gave Lucy a national reputation and her speaking engagements took her everywhere. Women's rights had become THE topic in the half of the population without them.

In her personal life, Lucy continued to march to her own drummer. For an extended period she adopted the controversial pant-skirt -- slacks worn under a shortened dress -- which had been popularized by Amelia . . . *Bloomer.* When she refused to pay taxes on her home because, without the vote, that constituted taxation without representation, her town seized her belongings and sold them at auction. And she continued the single life because existing laws, in her mind, would have reduced her to little more than a possession of her husband.

After two years of wooing, however, Henry Blackwell changed that. The entire Blackwell family -- three generations of them -- was committed to women's rights. Possibly because of that, Lucy relented, proceeding to the altar with Henry in 1855. Like Elizabeth Stanton and her husband, the couple omitted any reference to obedience in the marriage vows. Going one-up on Stanton, however, Lucy retained her maiden name. Those copying her lead were called "Lucy Stoners" or just "stoners" for decades.

Of her two children, only firstborn (1857) Alice Stone Blackwell survived, becoming a feminist leader in her own right.

As the 1861-1865 Civil War drew near, Lucy Stone had established herself as a national leader in both the abolition and women's rights movements. The Civil War would take her one step toward the realization of one of her goals, emancipation.

Susan B. Anthony (1820-1906)

As Lucretia Mott had invigorated the younger Elizabeth Cady Stanton, Stanton recruited and energized the younger Susan B. Anthony, who became the best-known of all the suffragettes. ("Suffragist" refers to persons of either sex; "suffragette" refers to a female suffragist.) Some have called Anthony the Napoleon of the movement. The half-century working relationship between her and Stanton is unprecedented in the annals of any U.S. reform movement. They were friends, partners, collaborators and confidants, and were there for each other during their many "down" periods.

Born in Massachusetts, Susan and her parents gradually moved westward, finally settling in Rochester, New York. She was a precocious child, learning to read and write in her pre-school years. Her father, upset with the snail-paced public school system, arranged for her education at home until she was old enough to complete her schooling at a Philadelphia Quaker boarding school.

Susan's father was a free-thinking Quaker who occasionally scandalized even his relatively liberal Hicksite group, the same group Lucretia Mott belonged to. He married a non-Quaker and enjoyed dancing. Like Mott, he became active in abolition and temperance movements.

Like Mott's father, he fostered independence in his children, male and female alike.

Following her father's lead, Susan learned to dance and developed an un-Quaker-like appreciation of fine clothes. Although she had suitors, she relished the independence of being single, which she remained throughout her life.

Like Lucretia Mott and Lucy Stone, Susan began teaching in her mid-teens, continuing in that role for 13 years. Like them, she resented earning a fraction of her male colleagues' salaries. This injustice sensitized her to the economic bonds that virtually enslaved women at the time, a lifelong concern of hers.

In 1848, Susan's parents and sister attended the Seneca Falls Woman's Rights Convention, returning with glowing accounts of Elizabeth Cady Stanton and Lucretia Mott. Anthony had not yet crystallized her views on women's rights and made no immediate effort to involve herself in any movement.

In 1851, however, the 31 year-old Anthony visited her friend, Amelia Bloomer, in Seneca Falls. While there, she attended an anti-slavery convention held by William Lloyd Garrison who had befriended Mott and Stanton in 1840 London and had hired Lucy Stone in Massachusetts. When Anthony met Stanton during the trip, the two developed an instantaneous bond that lasted five decades.

In the early 1850s, Susan's causes included abolition, temperance, women's dress reform, equal pay for male and female teachers and last, but not least, women's rights. She learned quickly that her sex was not an asset. When she was denied the right to speak at a temperance meeting, she and Stanton organized a women's temperance network throughout New York. Men quickly took over and even denied women the right to hold office in the very organization they had founded.

Demeaning as that experience was, it did give Anthony a network of colleagues around the state and, more importantly, provided her an opportunity to develop organizational skills which would become her lifelong *forte*.

Susan also witnessed the demise for lack of funds of many of the local temperance groups she had founded. This observation, coupled with her longtime concern about lack of equal pay for female teachers, consolidated her conviction that economic bondage nullified any realistic chance for equality for women. She wrote in her diary:

> **Woman must have a purse of her own and how can this be as long as the wife is denied the right to her individual and joint earnings. Reflections like these caused me to see and really feel that there was no true freedom for Woman without the possession of all her property rights, and that these rights could be obtained through legislation only, and so, the sooner the demand was made of the Legislature, the sooner would we be likely to obtain them. (Hymowitz and Weissman, p. 116)**

Stanton gave Susan B. Anthony the opportunity to do something about it. Elizabeth had long been associated with efforts to reform New York laws, especially those that forbade married women to own property or keep their own wages.

Although Elizabeth Cady Stanton was usually the one who started things, another woman -- fascinating in her own right -- got there first in regard to property rights.

Ernestine Rose, who started her life as a Jew in Poland and finished it as a social activist in England, invested her middle years in political activism in New York. More than a dozen years before the Seneca Falls convention, various bills had been introduced in the state legislature on women's property rights. Initially, it was mainly Rose who stomped the state, gathering signed petitions in favor. With time, Stanton and others joined her, resulting in the passage of the state's Married Women's Property Rights Act of 1848.

The act was only a small step in the right direction. It permitted women to keep property inherited before their marriages and to protect it from their husbands' debts. The next step, in the eyes of Rose and Stanton, would consist of protecting wages earned by married women, which legally belonged to their husbands.

Susan B. Anthony joined the cause at the right time. Effective as Rose had been, she also alienated many people in a variety of ways. Her immigrant status, her Jewish heritage, her sex and her apparent atheism all worked against her. Stanton, active though she was with the pen, was homebound in a perpetual state of pregnancy. The cause needed a mobile, socially acceptable person to comb the state in search of support.

Anthony filled the bill. She developed a brilliant, state-wide canvassing plan to solicit signed petitions in favor of a revised women's property law. In 1854, thousands of petitions were submitted to the legislature, but the legislators considered it a joke. More petitions were submitted the following year and Stanton spoke before the Joint Judiciary Committee. Again, they were laughed out of the legislature.

Exhausted from her travels and depressed by the failures, Susan reached a crossroad in her relationships. Was it fair for her to do it all? She had looked to Lucy Stone for help, but Lucy had just had a child. Distraught, Susan wrote Stanton that they (Stanton and Stone) have "given yourself over to baby-making, and left poor, brainless me to do battle alone." Whereas Elizabeth Stanton handled the situation sympathetically, Lucy Stone snapped back. From that time on, Susan maintained her warm relationship with Stanton, but remained cool toward Stone.

Stanton was the creative thinker, the philosopher and the gifted writer. Anthony was the Field Marshall, an organizational genius on the go. Stanton wrote the speeches; Anthony delivered them. Susan visited Elizabeth's home so frequently that the children called her Aunt Susan. They complemented each other perfectly. Although Anthony gradually became the greater force for change, she always credited Stanton with founding the women's rights movement, and she nearly always served as vice-president under president Stanton in their various organizations.

Despite early setbacks, Stanton, Anthony and Rose continued lobbying in the New York legislature. Finally in 1860, a bill passed that expanded a married woman's property rights, her right to sue, her right to joint custody of children and her right to make contracts. Most gratifying of all, wages from her work belonged to her. It was a smashing victory that served as a prototype for other states. If Stanton and Anthony had retired then, they still would have commanded a secure spot in history.

But they were just beginning, especially the irrepressible Stanton. Not content to rest on her laurels, Elizabeth introduced the topic of marriage and divorce at the 1860 annual women's rights convention. Just as she had been one step ahead of her peers on the subject of suffrage in 1848, so also her views on liberalizing divorce laws -- mild by today's standards -- made waves in an otherwise supportive assemblage. Although her pioneering thoughts brought great pain to Elizabeth throughout her life, they also controlled the feminist agenda by bringing to debate the thorny issues no one else dared touch.

Stanton's notion of marriage between equals was less startling to the conventioneers than her views on liberalizing divorce laws. The dominant opinion at the time held that divorce was contrary to God's law and even horribly bad marriages should remain intact.

Stanton's views split the convention. She did receive some support from women in temperance societies who had long advocated legalizing divorce from drunken, abusive husbands. The backlash, however, came from some key individuals.

The feminists never knew what to expect from abolitionist Wendell Phillips. He had been lukewarm in his support of Stanton and Lucretia Mott in London at the 1840 World Anti-Slavery Convention, but had supported women's rights generally and Elizabeth Stanton personally since then. At this convention he tried to table the subjects of equality in marriage and more liberal divorce laws, saying it was inappropriate for a women's rights convention. Lucy Stone sided with Phillips, possibly out of loyalty to her abolitionist associates.

The Reverend Antoinette Brown Blackwell, Lucy Stone's sister-in-law, defended from Scripture the image of a "true ideal of marriage," which should remain intact. Ernestine Rose sided with Stanton, arguing that Rev. Blackwell considered only what marriage should be, not what it frequently was. Susan B. Anthony and Lucretia

Mott also sided with Stanton. Powerful journalist Horace Greeley did not.

Lack of consensus was threatening the core of the feminist movement. Rival camps seemed to be emerging. Personal relationships were becoming strained. Fortunately for the movement, the Civil War provided a rallying position for the leaders. Nearly all of the feminists had also been active in the abolition movement, and the war offered the hope of emancipation.

Still, some of the wounds continued to fester. Stanton, some time later, wrote to Anthony: "Our religion, laws, customs are all founded on the belief that woman was made for man." It was a concern that she would take to the grave.

Sojourner Truth (c. 1797-1883)

The major actors who would dominate the women's rights stage for several decades had made their appearance: Lucretia Mott, Elizabeth Cady Stanton, Lucy Stone and Susan B. Anthony. But a host of others contributed significantly now and then, here and there in the pre-Civil War period. None was more colorful, more completely unique than Sojourner Truth. Just as Ernestine Rose had been one of the few early feminists of Jewish heritage, Sojourner almost alone represented the black woman.

Named Isabella at birth, her childhood was typical of too many enslaved children on Anglo-American plantations in the Deep South. Deprived of any education. Auctioned and sold several times. Forced to work long hours. Whipped at the slightest provocation. Living in unspeakably squalid and crowded conditions. Adulthood brought more of the same plus a forced "breeding" marriage that produced at least five children. Some died and some were sold into slavery away from her.

The major difference was, it wasn't in the Deep South. It was north of New York City and a little south of Elizabeth Stanton's childhood home. And her first owners were Dutch. After Isabella's sale from the Dutch family to English-speaking Americans, her whippings for disobedience were probably due to her limited understanding of English. (Her parents were most likely brought from Africa, but the record is not clear.)

At about 30 years of age, what type of woman would one expect to find after such treatment? Illiterate? Physically spent? Emotionally cowed? Devoid of hope? Defeated and submissive? Bitterly hateful of whites?

Illiterate, yes. No to all the rest. She was tall (about six feet) and wiry-strong. Self-confident. Blessed with a wry sense of humor and a love of singing with a deep, almost masculine voice. Determined. God-fearing, but fearful of nothing or no one else. Inner-directed. Most surprising of all, she felt a need to convince whites to atone for their sins against blacks, not to seek revenge against them.

Clearly not a product of her environment, Isabella was in every sense a self-made person -- self-made in personality, beliefs, attitudes, self-image and convictions, and she shared an important attribute with Lucretia Mott. Both drew strength from their religious beliefs, unlike some other suffragettes whose beliefs were compromised by their unsupportive, sometimes obstructive, denominations.

An 1810 New York law required the phasing in of emancipation, to be completed by 1828. A year before her emancipation, Isabella ran away. According to one story, she bolted when her owner failed to give her an early release in return for extra hard work. Another version has it that she left on direct orders from God.

For whatever reason, she made it to the Quaker home of Maria and Isaac Van Wagenen, with whom she stayed for several years. They bought the remaining year of her servitude and freed her. At long, long last, the independent spirit of Isabella was legally free after 30 years of demeaning existence. She adopted the Van Wagenen name and worshipped with them. To the astonishment of all, she took the offensive. With the help of the Quaker community, she sued her former owner who had sold her son into slavery in Alabama, in violation of New York law. Incredibly, she won the return of her son, thus becoming the first black person to sue whites successfully.

With her son and a fully ripened dedication to God, she moved to New York City, where she worked as a domestic and spent her free time preaching on street corners. She became a Methodist because "the Quakers wouldn't let me sing." For the rest of her life, freedom included singing any time she pleased, any place she pleased, any song she pleased. Although illiterate, she committed to memory long hymns and extensive Biblical passages.

In her mid-forties in 1843 and with her son off to sea on a whaling ship, Isabella finally embarked on her life's work. She was convinced that her God-given mission was to travel the land as a preacher, making whites face up to their sins against her people. Needing a name befitting her new role in life, she became Sojourner Truth, by which history knows her. Her first evangelical venture took her to New England, where she supported herself with odd jobs, frequently sleeping outdoors on the ground. She encountered many abolitionists along the way. Frederick Douglass, impressed with her oratory, influenced her toward the cause, but it's not entirely clear who influenced whom more.

Sojourner's popularity exploded in 1850, in her early fifties, when she published her autobiography, ghost written for her by a white woman, Olive Gilbert. In that year, she attended Lucy Stone's national women's rights convention in Massachusetts. From that time on, women's rights and abolitionism were inseparable causes.

Emotionally recharged and armed with a crate of her books to sell, Sojourner headed west, eventually buying a small house in Battle Creek, Michigan. Although she continued to travel the country, Battle Creek remained her home base.

Although her home-spun oratory and book had made her famous, Sojourner's boldest imprint on history came in 1851 in Akron, Ohio, at a women's rights convention. Her impromptu "Ain't I a Woman?" speech electrified the crowd and received national media coverage.

Only three years old, the women's rights movement had changed in mood as had the public's attitude toward it. It was no longer pioneering Lucretia Mott and Elizabeth Cady Stanton in tiny Seneca Falls or long-suffering Lucy Stone in Massachusetts. Those were the pebbles that rippled throughout the nation's pond, infecting dissatisfied women and open-minded men with enthusiastic zeal. It had become a full-scale, nationwide movement almost overnight. It was unorganized at first, but the groundswell of support had begun.

The male-dominated society had greeted the first conventions with detached derision. When it became clear that the notion of sexual equality was not about to die a quick, natural death, derision yielded to threat and anger. Many men attended the mushrooming number of local convocations, not just to laugh at the spectacle, but to yell down and intimidate assemblages of women with dangerous ideas.

Such was the case in Akron. It was strictly a local affair with none of the national leaders in attendance. Presiding president Frances Gage described the momentous event:

> **The second day the work waxed warm. Methodist, Baptist, Episcopal, Presbyterian, and Universalist ministers came in to hear and discuss the resolutions . . . . There were very few women in those days who dared to "speak in meeting"; and the august teachers of the people were seemingly getting the better of us, while the boys in the galleries, and the sneerers among the pews, were hugely enjoying (our) discomfiture . . . .the atmosphere betokened a storm. When slowly from her seat in the corner rose Sojourner Truth . . . . The tumult subsided at once, and every eye was fixed on this almost Amazon form, which stood nearly six feet high, head erect, and eyes piercing the upper air like one in a dream.**

(There are several accounts of Sojourner's short speech that day and all attempted to capture her unusual Dutch/English/Negro dialect, with limited success. I have eliminated most of it to focus more clearly on her message.)

Although the white women in attendance were reserved about speaking in public and nearly totally intimidated by a solid wall of opposing men of the cloth, Sojourner was not impressed at all. Addressing herself to one particular minister, she demonstrated once more, as she had done often before, an uncanny knack for knocking the high and mighty off their little pedestals.

> That little man in black there, he says women
> can't have as much rights as men because Christ
> wasn't a woman! Where did your Christ come
> from? (*She repeated the question with a rising
> voice.*) Where did your Christ come from? From
> God and a woman! Man had nothing to do with
> Him.

The approving crowd applauded wildly and continued cheering after nearly every sentence.

Although reports are somewhat conflicting, apparently some men in attendance had alluded to the chivalrous aid men offered to ladies at the time. In response to them, Sojourner launched her most frequently quoted tirade.

> That man over there says that women needs to
> be helped into carriages and lifted over ditches
> and have the best place everywhere. Nobody
> ever helps me into carriages or over mud
> puddles or gives me any best places. And ain't I a
> woman? Look at me. . . . I have ploughed and
> planted and gathered into barns . . . . And ain't I
> a woman? . . . I have seen most of my children
> sold into slavery . . . and none but Jesus heard
> me. And ain't I a woman?

Frances Gage summarized the reaction of the crowd.

> Amid roars of applause, (Sojourner) returned to
> her corner, leaving more than one of us with
> streaming eyes . . . . She had taken us up in her
> strong arms and (turned) the whole tide in our

favor. I have never in my life seen anything like the magical influence that subdued the mobbish spirit of the day and turned the sneers and jeers of an excited crowd into notes of respect and admiration.

In one fell swoop, Sojourner highlighted the rift in the religious community re: women's rights, the unconscionable snobbery of most men toward the cause and the omission of the black woman in the debate, and everyone loved her for it.

Sojourner Truth. Remarkable.

*   *   *

The early leaders of the feminist movement had little in common. They came from different religious backgrounds. Different socioeconomic circumstances. Ernestine Rose and Sojourner Truth constituted a minority representation of Jews and blacks. Not all married. Only some had supportive families.

However, all were also committed to the abolitionist cause and the Civil War was at hand. Would the war deliver the long-awaited freedom and equality for slaves? Could the women's rights movement sustain its momentum though a prolonged war? The future was far from clear.

Chapter 4

1860-1870: War, Conflict, Defeat and Division

What do you do when you work so effectively that your job is given to a member of the opposite sex, just because that person *is* of the opposite sex?

That was the dilemma facing Clara Barton just before the Civil War. Like so many girls at that time, she began teaching in her teens because it was one of the few occupations available to persons of her gender. She excelled at it year after year, but her considerable organizational skills gradually begged for a new challenge. When the opportunity came to rescue a school struggling with underenrollment, she jumped at the chance. But when she accomplished what she was hired to do -- fill the school -- the local officials were so pleased they gave her job to a male. Should Clara accept the demotion gracefully?

She wasn't the first woman faced with such a dilemma. Massachusetts' Lucy Stone had done so well at liberal Oberlin College that she was invited to write a commencement speech. *Write* it. It would be read by a male student. Lucy refused.

Susan B. Anthony was not allowed to speak at a temperance conference because she was a woman, so she started her own state-wide network of women's temperance organizations. Liberal males were so impressed that they took over and barred women from holding office. Susan invested her time elsewhere.

If liberal, educated, progressive men treated highly talented women so callously, what was the fate of untold tens of thousands of women at the hands of "conservative" males? Most simply accepted the humiliation and disappeared from the annals of recorded history. Others such as Lucy Stone and Susan B. Anthony made reforming the repressive system their lives' work. Some others simply kicked open the doors of opportunity and succeeded in spite of the discrimination: Clara Barton was one of those. She did not make women's rights her life's work, but her pioneering life and the lives of those like her gave plausibility to the women's rights movement. She and they were living proof that women deserved more than second class citizenship.

After leaving the school in protest of her demotion, Barton ventured to Washington, D.C. Her job in the U.S. Patent Office made her one of the first women in federal employ.

With the outbreak of the Civil War in 1861, restrictive social conventions were relaxed in support of an all-out war effort. In such an environment, the then middle-aged Barton advertised for medical supplies and food, which she delivered directly to the battlefields in Maryland and Virginia. She also provided some battlefield nursing services, the first of her gender to do so under combat conditions. Her fame as the "angel of the battlefield" spread quickly throughout the news-starved North.

Toward the war's end, Clara started an agency to locate the remains of 10,000 missing Union troops. Her organizational skills amazed all who knew her. Having depleted her personal savings to support her work, Barton went on a grueling lecture tour to replenish her bank account. In so doing, she became a well-known inspiration and role model for countless women seeking a way out of a subservient lifestyle. Later, she showed the way again by founding the American Red Cross, which is still serving the country.

Thousands of others in women's auxiliaries for the war effort gained organizational skills, confidence and networks of contacts that would serve other purposes in years to come. With the men at war, jobs opened to women and the remnants of social stigma attached to traveling without male escort and to public speaking all but disappeared.

On the Back Burner

The women's rights leaders put their agenda on hold and joined the war effort in a variety of ways. Sojourner Truth left her home in Michigan to volunteer in several programs in the Washington, D.C. area. While there, she made her last major contribution to the women's rights cause, and racial justice as well. Twice conductors in the capital's trolley system refused to let Sojourner board. She suffered a dislocated shoulder and bruises when one of the conductors refused to stop for her, dragging her as she tried to hold on. Her subsequent suit led directly to the desegregation of the trolley system in Washington, a monumental achievement for the times and another first for Sojourner.

She was approaching 70 as the war ended and remained as active as she could, but spent more and more time at her Michigan home. Even her death in 1883 was noteworthy. She was attended by a physician interested in the nutritional value of breakfast cereals, Dr. John Kellogg of

Battle Creek, Michigan. No African-American woman during or after Sojourner's lifetime had a greater impact on the woman's rights/suffrage movement.

Sojourner Truth! A legend in her own time who left very large footprints in the sand.

Meanwhile, Lucretia Mott, opposed to the war on religious grounds, invested time in the 1864 founding of Swarthmore College for young Quaker men and women. She also ministered to the needs of black troops being trained near her home.

Stone, Anthony and Stanton gravitated, as usual, to the top of the largest national association supporting the war effort, the Loyal League. The Stantons had moved to the New York City area, a vast improvement over Elizabeth's isolation in remote Seneca Falls. With Susan B. Anthony on salary, the Loyal League networked itself nationally and presented to Congress over a quarter-million petitions for a constitutional end to slavery.

Although most people today equate the Civil War with the end of slavery, many in the North at the time supported the war to preserve the union, not necessarily to free the slaves. And many of those who favored abolition preferred phasing slavery out over a long period. Consequently, reformers felt the need to keep the heat on politicians to assure at least some progress for the slaves, hopefully total abolition at once.

The high point of the Civil War from the reformers' perspective, therefore, was President Lincoln's Emancipation Proclamation. It read in part:

> . . . on (day of the proclamation), all persons held as slaves within any State or designated part of a

State the people whereof shall then be in rebellion against the United States shall be then, thenceforward and forever free . . . .

Not all persons realize that the proclamation came in the middle of the war, not at the beginning, and that only slaves in the rebelling states were freed, not slaves in some Union states. The delayed proclamation and its limited application were intended to keep support for the war high in the North until the outcome was no longer in question.

With the war over, however, and with obstreperous representatives from the South gone from Washington, Congress could not permit slavery in the states that had at least tacitly fought for its abolition. On December 18, 1865, therefore, the Thirteenth Amendment to the Constitution passed. It stated simply:

Neither slavery nor involuntary servitude, except as a punishment for a crime whereof the party shall have been convicted, shall exist within the United States, or any place subject to their jurisdiction.

At last, freedom had finally been substituted for slavery. Yet, freedom did not guarantee equality of rights, and reformers considered the job only half-done. And they agreed the most important single right was the right to vote.

Suffrage then became the goal of "abolitionists" and feminists alike, for slaves and women together. They joined forces in the new American Equal Rights Association with Lucretia Mott, a leader in both movements, the president.

At this juncture, the women's rights movement noticeably shifted its philosophy. It had borrowed its initial battle cry from the Declaration of Independence's call to protect God-given rights. And its early reform efforts targeted public opinion and politicians at the state level. And with the religious community withholding its support and with the emergence of the federal government as a stronger level of government, the emphasis shifted from God-given rights to rights of citizenship and from state-level activism to state- *and* national-level activism. Anthony was the first to recognize the emerging federal role. The failure of other suffragettes to do so helped pave the way for future friction.

The relationship between the male abolitionists and the feminists also began to erode. Although, in the giddiness of the successful Civil War and the Thirteenth Amendment's passage, they agreed to work together for the simultaneous enfranchisement of freed slaves and women, the abolitionists had second thoughts. Support for Negro suffrage was far from universal and adding the equally controversial issue of woman suffrage placed the outcome of black-rights activism in even greater jeopardy. To finish the job that emancipation had started, therefore, they preferred to seek black suffrage first, woman suffrage later. More and more of them referred to the "Negro hour" as their first priority. Feminist leaders, initially shocked at this shift in position, took no immediate action.

Lucretia Mott tried valiantly to hold the two sides together, but advancing age and infirmity were taking their toll. Reluctantly and silently, the prime mover of the feminist movement gradually retreated into the obscurity of advanced age.

Early Tests, Both Federal and State

The half-dozen years following the Civil War settled the relationship between abolitionists and feminists and mapped the future of the woman's rights movement. The defining issues were two constitutional amendments at the national level and three tests at the state/territory level. They coincided as follows:

> 1867 - Kansas test
> 1868 - Fourteenth Amendment
> 1869 - Wyoming test
> 1870 - Fifteenth Amendment
> 1870 - Utah test

Debate on the Fourteenth Amendment preceded the Kansas test. The amendment was crucial not only because it intended to enfranchise freed slaves, but also because, for the first time, the federal government defined "voter" for the states, a right theretofore reserved by the states. The wordy amendment's principal provisions were:

> **All persons born or naturalized in the United States . . . are citizens of the United States and of the State wherein they reside.. . . But when the right to vote is denied to any of the male inhabitants of such State (Congressional representation shall be reduced proportional to the degree of denial).**

It was a mixed blessing for females and contained a loophole for disenfranchising black males.

Clearly women were recognized as citizens and hopefully, therefore, entitled to all the privileges of citizenship, which were not spelled out. But the somewhat clear, somewhat ambiguous reference to male voters shocked the feminists. Apparently a state could deny women the right to vote without penalty! And if a state were willing to sacrifice some Congressional representation in order to disenfranchise black males, it could do so -- clearly not Congressional intent. And a state could apparently disenfranchise freed black females without penalty, but not freed black males.

The ambiguities and contradictions were so immediately apparent that debate on a new amendment began even before the fourteenth had been fully ratified.

Meanwhile, one state and two territories west of the Mississippi were taking matters into their own hands without regard to the mess in the nation's capital. Paradoxically, eastern suffrage leaders worked one of the three tests exhaustively and lost; they ignored the other two and woman suffrage won.

Suffragists and abolitionists alike rejoiced when Kansas brought to referendum in 1867 both black and woman suffrage. It was reputed to be a liberal state with political leaders favorable to both suffrages. To help, Lucy Stone and husband Henry Blackwell arrived first in the spring of 1867, joined by Elizabeth Cady Stanton and Susan B. Anthony in September. (Stanton's youngest child was eight and this was the first of her many trips from home, freed at last from daily child care duties.) Other eastern suffragettes trickled in to help garner public opinion, gather petitions and generally help out. All went well at first.

However, whereas the suffragettes worked for both black and woman suffrage, the abolitionists nearly to a man refused to work actively for woman suffrage. They believed the "Negro hour," as they called it, was hard enough to sell without burdening it with the equally convoluted issue of woman suffrage. Opponents of one or both suffrages used a hostile press to exaggerate the differences between the reform groups, with the result that neither won. Negro suffrage received only a third of the votes and woman suffrage, a little less than that. Exhausted by the ordeal and furious at the unsupportive abolitionists, the eastern suffragettes trudged home in disarray.

The subsequent ratification of the Fourteenth Amendment in 1918 reversed the Kansas referendum, however, so that at least the black male had the vote there and in the other states as well.

Meanwhile, a woman suffrage bill was quietly gaining momentum in the Wyoming Territory, coming to vote in 1869. With almost no national fanfare before or after its passage, Wyoming became the first jurisdiction, albeit a territory rather than a state, to fully enfranchise its women. Indeed, it received so little attention that there are several competing stories about how it came to pass.

The genteel version maintains that frontier men, caring little for eastern customs and holding their spouses in high regard, simply shared the vote out of a sense of respect.

A less rosy version holds that the Democratic Party leaders, assured that the Republican governor would veto an unpopular bill, passed it to embarrass him. But the equally conniving governor outfoxed them by signing it.

An even less rosy version holds that the white male establishment feared that westward-bound hordes of ex-slaves, Civil War veterans, brawling Irishmen and Chinese railroad workers would swamp the tiny resident population, wresting political control from it. Since most of these fortune seekers were bachelors, giving wives the right to vote effectively and protectively doubled the established electorate.

For whatever reason or combination of reasons, the bill passed. National celebrations were few, however, and again for a variety of reasons. First, the established leaders of the suffrage movement had contributed nothing to the victory. Secondly, Wyoming was a territory, not a state, and had an almost negligible population. Thirdly, suffrage leaders were still licking their wounds from the Kansas defeat and the insult of the Fourteenth Amendment. And fourthly, everyone was totally obsessed with the emerging Fifteenth Amendment.

Meanwhile, in 1870, the Utah Territory was following in Wyoming's footsteps. The resident Mormon population, definitely threatened by the waves of eastern fortune seekers, gave their women the vote to maintain political control. Eastern suffragettes, offended by the Mormon practice of polygamy, felt little joy over the victory there.

Unheralded suffragettes in the surrounding states did rejoice, however, and suffrage flourished first in the West as eastern hard-liners, pro and con, fought each other to a standstill decade after decade.

At long last, the Fifteenth Amendment arrived in 1870. The major provisions in the tersely worded amendment were:

The right of citizens of the United States to vote shall not be denied or abridged on account of race, color, or previous condition of servitude.

Wham! No Constitutional protection for the civil rights of women. The deliberate omission placed the ball right back in the state court in regard to suffrage. Combining the Fourteenth and Fifteenth Amendments, the black male was fully enfranchised. Women, black and white, were in limbo.

When the Fifteenth Amendment had been initially proposed, Elizabeth Cady Stanton and Susan B. Anthony revolted. Both felt they could not, in good conscience, support the passage and ratification of an amendment that, by omission, deprived women of the right to vote in recalcitrant states. Given that, they also could no longer tolerate the plea from male abolitionists to wait their turn because it was the "Negro hour." They decided to try to marshal the feminist movement *against* the passage and ratification of the Fifteenth Amendment.

Lucy Stone was in a quandary. Abolitionists had made her career possible. Reluctantly, she leaned toward supporting the amendment since at least it was a partial victory for civil rights.

Unity of Goal, Organizational Division

Stanton and Anthony left Stone no alternative with their next action. Stating that men had suppressed women at home, at church, in the work place, in government and even in reform organizations, it was time for women to fly on their own. The two leaders separated from the American Equal Rights Association, forming an all-woman *National* Woman Suffrage Association.

Since Henry Blackwell, Lucy's husband, had worked as hard as any woman for women's rights, the exclusion of him and other male supporters was unconscionable for her. As a counter move, Stone formed the *American* Woman Suffrage Association. The split into two feminist camps was complete. The organizational divorce between abolitionists and suffragists was complete. It was a new era.

Interestingly, one thing still united the two feminist camps, at least in spirit. The word "suffrage" appeared in the titles of both organizations. In 1848, at the start of the women's rights movement at the Seneca Falls conference, only suffrage had divided those in attendance because it was unthinkably absurd. Twenty-two years later, it was THE issue that united in spirit even rival groups. Suffrage had become the *sine qua non* of the women's rights movement. Even so, 50 more years of agony remained. So polarized and stalemated had the country become that many other countries around the world would grant woman suffrage before the United States of America, land of the free and home of the brave.

Without the guidance, support and protection of the male abolitionists, their money and their organizations, women were forced to negotiate their own way through an unsympathetic, male-dominated society. And it was a rough-and-tumble, rapidly changing society, indeed.

Chapter 5

Gridlock: 1870-1899 --
the Context

By 1870, the suffrage movement was developing a life of its own. Nearly half the women alive could not remember a time without discussion of women's rights in general and suffrage in particular. Before that, a woman's self-identity was limited to her immediate family and her church, and determined by them. By 1870 a broader identity of womanhood was emerging, linking all members of that gender in an unprecedented way. For the first time, nearly every woman had, or was developing, a conscious attitude toward the role of women in society, its ideal and its reality, and they derived that attitude from . . . women.

The gradual swelling of the wave of feminist activism, however, did not develop in a vacuum. Vast social and economic changes were unfolding in the century's last thirty years. Some created a favorable environment for the advancement of women and others constrained it. None had a greater impact than the industrial revolution and its consequences, particularly urbanization. Migration, agrarian in the West but urban in the East and Midwest, simultaneously changed the American scene.

Industrialization, Urbanization and Migration

In the U.S. as in Europe, industrialization began in the eighteenth century and accelerated rapidly throughout the nineteenth. In the U.S., industrialization proceeded much more rapidly in the Northeast and Midwest than in the South, giving Union states an insurmountable advantage over the South in the Civil War.

Industrialization meant larger and larger organizations for processing raw materials and manufacturing goods for sale. That, in turn, required an ever-growing labor force which, in turn, resulted in urbanization - the concentration of many persons in one locality near places of employment. Although much of rural farm families' production was for their own consumption, the urban family purchased with money the goods and services it needed. That, in turn, supported the growth of family owned businesses and fee-for-service professionals, such as doctors and lawyers. Urban life and rural life began to differ in more and more ways.

The data below demonstrate just how massive and rapid urbanization was. In the half-century from 1850 to 1900, the country's total population more than doubled. However, the rate of growth in urban areas was 2.5 times more rapid than in rural areas.

That's astounding, considering the westward flow of the population in search of farmland. In 1800, the statistical center of the population was near Baltimore; in 1850, West Virginia; in 1870, Ohio; in 1900, Indiana. The lands west of the Mississippi River had been acquired by purchase or conquest in the first half of the eighteenth century and settled largely in the second half. Waves of settlers rolled westward in pursuit of seemingly unlimited free land.

With so many Easterners heading west for an agricultural life, where did all the people come from to populate the East's urban areas? Immigration from Europe was a prime

Population in Millions

Year	total	urban	% urban
1850	23.2	3.5	15%
1870	38.6	-	-
1900	76.0	30.1	40%

factor. In 1850, 9.7 percent of the population was foreign-born; by 1900, 13.6 percent. (The two percentages are nearly additive since most of the foreign-born residents in 1850 had died by 1900.) With the exception of English-speaking Irish, the immigrants' cultures differed significantly from the established population of English descent. Jewish and Catholic immigrants were especially "different."

The new urban lifestyle dramatically changed the family and gender-specific roles within it. In the traditional small family business and on family farms, the men, women, children and extended family members all lived together and worked together -- all day, every day. In cities, the homeplace and the workplace were separated. The male left home to earn living capital; hours were long and a six-day work-week was usual. By default, nearly all domestic duties fell to the female. Compared to today, the number of children was large and life expectancy, short, so that child care consumed most of the average female's adult life.

Working class and middle class lifestyles in 1870 differed considerably in the burgeoning cities. At the lower level, children went to work early with little or no education. Females continued to work until they married, after which child care and other household duties consumed the day. In the middle class, females were usually educated at least through junior high age; many went on to finishing schools and an ever-increasing number went to college. After marriage and childbearing, cheap immigrant help with domestic chores freed the wife for whatever she chose and her husband could afford. Cities offered a variety of cultural, educational, charitable and civic opportunities, and middle-class, Protestant wives sampled them freely.

In the urban areas of 1870, therefore, there was a sufficiently large number of relatively affluent women with the luxury of "free time" to allow those with similar interests to find each other and to meet easily and regularly. It was a circumstance unprecedented in our history, supportive of the formation of many types of women's groups and organizations.

A Changing Climate of Reform

From the founding of our country to the Civil War, the issue of slavery dominated the waking hours of most reformers almost to the exclusion of everything else. Almost. Quietly gaining momentum at the same time was the issue of intemperate drinking.

Wine and beer had been consumed since the dawn of civilization. In the eighteenth century, however, distilled spirits gained popularity both in Europe and the United States with a disastrous impact on sobriety. Indeed, the rum trade with Caribbean countries was a mainstay of our colonial economy, and the taxes from it were indispensable to local government.

Tobacco and alcohol were considered aids to good health at the time. Tobacco was thought to improve the lungs. Alcohol was used to treat everything from arthritis in adults to teething pain in infants. In battlefield hospitals, liquor was poured *onto* wounds as an antiseptic and *into* soldiers as an anesthetic. William and Mary College even ran its own brewery for the students.

With the colonies fairly aglow, concerns about intemperance began to surface in the mid-1700s. Personages such as Washington and Franklin expressed concern, and religious groups became alarmed.

When the abolition movement began to flourish in the early 1800s, local temperance societies also appeared. Religious groups strongly supported them and men controlled them. Women were either silent supporters or members of an auxiliary. As time passed, "temperance" gradually became nearly synonymous with prohibition.

Maine became the first state to enact "partial option" laws that allowed local jurisdictions to control the production, transportation and sale of alcoholic beverages within their boundaries. In the two decades before the Civil War, over a dozen states enacted and repealed, enacted and repealed, enacted and repealed all sorts of measures to return their citizenries to sobriety. The cumulative efforts were partially successful as seen in the drop in per capita consumption from an astounding seven gallons of pure alcohol per person in the 1820s to two gallons in 1855.

During the Civil War, most of those laws were repealed or went unenforced; the Union needed the alcohol tax for the war effort. After the war and the enfranchisement of freed slaves, abolition no longer commanded center stage for reform-minded persons, thereby exposing intemperance as the next likely target.

The liquor industry correctly assumed that it was in a fight for survival. At the National Brewers' Congress in 1867, the members openly espoused a policy of defeating temperance candidates at the polls. Reformers responded with the Prohibition (political) Party in 1869. From 1870 on, the fight -- brawl, actually -- raged.

The "saloon" became, for many, the principal symbol of evil in society, especially in the eyes of married women. In 1870, over 100,000 saloons served the country's men -- roughly one for every 400 men, women and children. They were readily accessible to whites and blacks (who adopted the white man's bad habits with startling alacrity), rich and poor, urban and rural -- even immigrants who brought their Old World drinking habits with them found solace in the neighborhood watering hole.

Women were appalled. Their men spent prodigious amounts of time there, squandered their meager wages, lost money and homes and farms gambling, were frequently injured or worse in barroom fights and came home in disgraceful shape. It just had to stop!

Less obvious to women of the times was the political clout wielded by and at the saloons. The millions of men who frequented them knew full well that those places of relaxation and comradery were under fire at the polls. The liquor industry recognized the voting power of the saloons' huge constituency and fed the patrons a continuous line of slurs, lies and spicy rumors about temperance candidates. Local political bosses routinely bought a round for the house as they molded political opinion. And with saloons open on election day, men flocked to them for free drinks provided by anti-temperance candidates. Indeed, the saloon industry was arguably the single most influential political institution in the country, unquestionably so in the matter of temperance issues.

No male temperance sympathizer would ever venture near a saloon. But the women did. In large numbers. In 1873. In a spontaneous uprising that has never been completely explained, groups of women all over the country began marching from churches to saloons, praying and singing hymns outside. It was an entirely unprecedented gender-to-gender confrontation.

Female memberships in the suffrage and temperance movements did overlap, but were basically quite distinct. Saloon-goers, however, made little distinction between the meddling ol' biddies in the suffrage movement and the sanctimonious Bible thumpers singing outside. If the suffragists won, the tipplers believed, enfranchised women would use the vote to close the saloons. That conclusion would cost the suffrage movement dearly in the decades ahead.

The dominance of a few, interrelated reform issues is reflected in the history of amendments to the Constitution. From 1865 to 1933, six of the nine amendments dealt with abolition (one), suffrage (three) and prohibition (two). (The other three were concerned with the income tax and general governmental operations.)

A Massive Coming Out

It is difficult today to understand just how difficult it was for colonial women to do anything on their own. They spent most of their time at home in interaction with husbands, children and extended family members. The family traveled together to church and to shop. Church-based activities were supervised by clergy*men* or elders. Unescorted travel by women was severely frowned upon and, in most rural areas, there was little to travel to, anyway. Although there was free speech, women were not expected to use it in public.

In the early 1800s, the proliferation of abolition and temperance societies did create opportunities for organizational membership, but women were generally relegated to helper roles or membership in auxiliaries. When the Seneca Falls conference was held in 1848, Lucretia Mott's husband was asked to chair it because none of the women knew how.

As travel taboos relaxed and industrialization and urbanization created a large number of women with leisure time, the setting was complete for some women, at least, to venture out on their own. As they did so and found others with similar interests, they began aggregating themselves into organizations. The most significant early ones became the cornerstone of the Women's Club Movement. In 1868, Julia Ward Howe help found the New England Women's Club and in New York City, Jane Croly helped found Sorosis. Other clubs quickly followed suit throughout the country.

These early clubs were study clubs for self-improvement. They especially filled a need among women who had had no college opportunities in their younger years. Equally importantly, they were "safe" to join. There was none of the intense controversy that surrounded suffrage or abolition organizations; no one objected to their studies of Greek literature or Japanese gardening. And even more importantly, they were organizations *for* women and run *by* women.

With time, the clubs expanded to civic improvement projects -- libraries, schools, playgrounds -- an impressive panoply of improvements. Although many men and some women poked fun at these new roles, they were still "safe."

By 1890, the General Federation of Women's Clubs gave a national identity to the over 5,000 known clubs.

In the formative years of the club movement, another opportunity for organizational membership arose, spontaneously at first. In 1873, groups of women began congregating outside saloons to pray and sing hymns. In 1874, Annie Wittenmyer used organizational experience gained during the Civil War to help found the Woman's Christian Temperance Union (WCTU). In five years, over 25,000 women in over 1,000 local organizations took aim on the liquor industry.

Membership in the WCTU was still "safe," but less so than in the club movement. The liquor industry was a formidable enemy and support in the home was frequently weak or non-existent. But it had the solid backing of the religious community and a significant part of the male population. The righteousness of the cause made some of the agonies of membership quite tolerable.

After Wittenmyer, Frances Willard led the WCTU into the next century, expanded membership into the hundreds of thousands and helped found the World WCTU in 1891. Her successors expanded membership to 800,000, whose cumulative pressure contributed to a prohibition amendment to the Constitution shortly before the suffragists did the same for their cause.

In addition to ever-expanding organizational opportunities for women, the pre-Civil War expansion of college and professional educational opportunities accelerated enormously. In 1800, a young woman dared not travel alone away from home but, it 1899, could not only travel to college alone, but live there, away from home, for years and without social censure.

It was a new world out there, and more and more women were venturing out into it. They were educating themselves, forcing open occupational opportunities, organizing themselves and creating an ever-expanding self-image for womanhood. Should they vote? Well, of course!

And Then There Was Suffrage . . . .

Membership in women's rights groups, expectedly, carried the greatest risk. The early affiliation of these groups with the abolition movement had assured at least some support from the liberal male community. After the Civil War, however, they were on their own and had targeted the most controversial goal of all, woman suffrage. A feeling began to emerge that, with the vote, women could redress all other grievances.

By 1870, the battle lines were drawn.

On the "anti" side, "male supremacists" reigned supreme. They ranged from macho men to kindly souls who genuinely wanted to care for the weaker sex, which included taking on the major responsibilities of life, like voting, for which they had greater aptitude. World-wide and history-long, they had considered themselves superior to women in everything except childbearing and home maintenance. Sharing the vote, they thought, would lead to frivolous government and social chaos.

The "liquor sector," overwhelmingly dominated by men, could depend on suffrage resistance from producers, distributors, saloon owners, political bosses dependent upon the booze vote, and conscientious tipplers *en masse.*

Major segments of the religious establishment, traditionally male, stood pat. Conservative interpretations of the Bible ascribed a submissive role to females both in church and in the family. The women's rights movement as a whole, in the eyes of many, threatened to destabilize both home and the church, to say nothing of society at large.

The entire South associated women's rights with abolition and the Union. Progress was slower there than in any part of the country.

Some women spoke out against suffrage. Although not numerous, they did allow the antis to claim there were still some sensible women left in the country.

The entire working class was largely indifferent to the issue. They were so preoccupied with poor working conditions, poor living conditions, discrimination and the daily struggle for survival that the suffrage cause seemed largely irrelevant to their lives. Immigrant groups, however, leaned toward opposing suffrage because most of them had come from patriarchal societies which had not even experienced a desensitizing shock such as the Seneca Falls conference and its aftermath.

On the mildly "pro" side was the large and ever growing ensemble of middle and upper class women, especially Protestant women in cities. They were excited about the changing self-image of womanhood and the expanding opportunities for women in society. If the vote were given to them, they would gladly accept it but, for most, becoming a visible activist risked too much opprobrium at home, at church and in their social networks. They rooted quietly from the sidelines for an entire generation.

The Quaker denomination led the larger Christian community by example. Gender equality in it was a fact. It contributed many leaders to the cause, most notably Lucretia Mott, Susan B. Anthony and, later, Alice Paul. It was, however, a small denomination with few admirers in the larger Christian community.

Middle class males with a sense of justice and/or exposure to competent women in their environments were generally supportive, but infrequently to the degree of activism.

The ever-growing, but still small, ranks of activists were composed mainly of middle-class, city-dwelling, risk-taking, Protestant women who believed their lot in life was what they made it. Joined by a few committed men, not led by them, they simply refused to take NO from the recalcitrant male establishment.

The anti forces clearly had the numbers, the wealth, the power, the tradition and the need to retain control. Only in the West did the pro and con forces come even close to parity. It is little wonder, then, that the burgeoning woman suffrage movement scored few major victories for an entire generation. It was a bit like trying to walk up the down escalator.

Forcing the Issue

There's a world of difference between not having the vote because that's the way it's always been and being deliberately snubbed by the highest legislative body in all the land with the support of most of the states in the land. The Fourteenth and Fifteenth Amendments to the Constitution sent a clear and simple snub to half the population -- women, you are citizens of these United States without the cardinal right of citizenship in a democracy, the right to vote!

Women all over the country marched to the polls at the next elections to challenge that insult. They tried to vote in

New Hampshire and D.C. and California and Illinois and Connecticut, to name just a few. And over and over, they were turned away. These were not the usual suffragettes. They also included ordinary, unaffiliated citizens who demanded the rights of citizenship.

The leaders, of course, also challenged at the polls and they commanded most of the media's attention. Aging Sojourner Truth still regaled everyone with her humorous one-upmanship. When an obstreperous official in Michigan denied her access to the voting booth and called her "auntie," she in turn referred to him as "nephew."

Susan B. Anthony had a larger agenda in mind. She was arrested after she tried to vote. An arrogant U.S. district judge refused to let her testify on her own behalf and fined her $100. She refused to pay, hoping to appeal the decision all the way to the Supreme Court. Fearing that, the authorities released her without collecting the fine.

A Supreme Court test did come in October of 1874 in *Minor v. Happersett*. Victoria Minor had sued the Missouri official, Happersett, who had denied her the vote. Her lawyer-husband argued the case all the way to the Supreme Court and . . . lost.

Gloom settled over the suffrage movement. The insult to one half of the country's population had become clearer than ever. They had been slapped down once more. They had no choice but to dig their heels into the deepening muck around them and prepare for the long haul. Men were not about to surrender their supremacy without a fight.

Only two strategies were available -- work to change suffrage laws state by state and/or lobby for an amendment to the Constitution. Although neither held much promise, there wasn't an ounce of quit in the movement. Half the slaves women had sacrificed fathers and husbands and sons to free in the war could vote. Half the immigrants they had welcomed into their land could vote. So, too, would they.

Chapter Appendix

Two Steps Backward

Although the principal suffrage leaders were remarkably free of scandal in their private lives, two lesser players gave the movement a black eye after the Civil War.

Victoria Woodhull galloped through the 1870s with an incredible outburst of enterprises – stock broker, spiritualist, newspaper publisher and self-appointed spokesperson for woman suffrage. Beautiful, articulate and ambitious, she became the first woman to testify before Congress for suffrage.

Stanton and Anthony invited Woodhull into their organization, but soon regretted it. Victoria publicly identified herself as a free-lover, frivolously declared her candidacy for the U.S. presidency and exposed an affair both suffrage organizations had tried to keep hidden.

The Rev. Henry Ward Beecher, brother of author Harriet Beecher Stowe, had been the first president of Lucy Stone's American WSA and also had had an affair with the wife of one of his parishioners. Woodhull exposed the affair in her newspaper and was promptly arrested for sending obscene literature through the mail. When the injured husband sued Beecher for alienation of affection, the nation's newspapers delighted in the story for months.

The double-barreled scandal smudged the suffragists' image for many years, to the delight of their foes.

Chapter 6

Gridlock: 1870-1899 --

Inch by Inch Progress

In the context of Chapter Five's content, we may return to the end of Chapter 4. When the abolitionists told the suffragettes after the Civil War that they would have to wait their turn, Susan B. Anthony and Elizabeth Cady Stanton bolted from the jointly sponsored American Equal Rights Association and formed the separate, all woman National Woman Suffrage Association (National WSA). Loyal to her abolition friends, but still deeply troubled by their attitude, Lucy Stone countered with the co-ed American WSA. And she took Julia Ward Howe with her as the first president of the new organization.

Howe, the daughter of a wealthy banker, had gained a modest reputation in pre-Civil War New England as a writer. During the war, a companion suggested she write new words for the tune, *John Brown's Body*. She did and her *Battle Hymn of the Republic* instantly became THE song of the Union, giving her near universal name recognition and respect in the North. Because of that, she became a welcome addition to the suffrage movement after the war and worked with Stone in Boston off and on for the rest of her long life. With Stone and others, she helped found the Association for the Advancement of Women in

1873 and later became the first president of the Massachusetts Federation of Women's Clubs. She also became an activist in international suffrage and peace movements.

Lucy Stone was the continuing force behind the American WSA for its 21-year existence and helped found a feminist periodical, *The Woman's Journal*. It was edited for two years by Mary Livermore who had developed organizational skills during the Civil War and used them for the suffrage cause in Illinois before moving to Boston. After the first two years, Stone edited it for the rest of her life, and her daughter thereafter, with occasional help from Julia Ward Howe and others. She sought and received literary contributions from personages such as Harriet Beecher Stowe and Louisa May Alcott. It became the unquestioned leading periodical for the women's rights movement for decades.

Unlike Anthony and Stanton, Stone favored a "bottom up" strategy in which local suffrage groups would enfranchise women state-by-state. The decision in *Minor v. Happersett* clarified that the Supreme Court did not consider voting an automatic right of citizenship, leaving that decision to each state. Given that, the Stone-led annual conferences of the American WSA were offered sequentially all over the country to spur local initiatives. It was a busy life for Lucy Stone, Howe and associates.

Elizabeth Cady Stanton also experienced a spurt of adrenaline, although extreme weight and failing eyesight would gradually slow her down. She went on the lucrative lecture tour for 11 years, becoming self-supporting for the first, delightfully rewarding time. She was witty, warm, provocative, persuasive, famous and in demand. Mostly, however, Stanton worked with Susan B. Anthony who outworked everyone for over three decades. Stanton, Anthony and Matilda Gage (not to be confused with

Frances Gage at the famous Akron convention) wrote the first three volumes of the *History of Woman Suffrage*. Stanton was nearly always the president of the National WSA with Anthony as vice-president, reversing their roles only once in the 21-year existence of the association. And, like Stone, Stanton and Anthony began their own periodical.

The periodical's name, *The Revolution*, was apropos. Compared to the more conservative *Woman's Journal*, it was racy and radical, embracing controversial topics such as divorce law reform. It also was undercapitalized, resulting in failure in a few years.

Although Stanton and Anthony worked together continuously and closely, their reference contexts drifted apart somewhat. Stanton had single-handedly forced the suffrage issue on the Seneca Falls convention attendees as a necessary component of a comprehensive women's rights package. Decades later, she was equally concerned that a preoccupation with suffrage would compromise the overall progress of women's rights. Her insistence on retaining controversial components of the package, such as divorce law reform, alienated many suffragettes, forcing them into the Lucy Stone camp, which was perceived as much more conservative and respectable.

Anthony's tunnel vision, in contrast, never wavered from suffrage. After *Minor v. Happersett*, she became convinced that the only sensible strategy was to lobby for an amendment to the Constitution. Time proved Stanton and Anthony right about nearly everything. The abolitionists never supported suffrage *en masse*, as they both had predicted. Stanton believed that enfranchisement alone would not, by itself, lead to the redress of all grievances; after receiving the vote after her death, women never voted as a bloc. And Anthony's belief proved true, that a state-by-state strategy was not the quickest road to victory, although it was a helpful ancillary strategy. Susan spent more and more time in Washington, lobbying for the amendment in her usual tireless manner.

Progress was slow at both the state and national levels for decades. In state after state, suffrage bills and referenda were routinely defeated, usually by a two-to-one margin. The liquor industry and the religious establishment, opposed to each other on temperance issues, constituted a formidable one-two punch in favor of male supremacy.

The suffragette leaders stumped state after state with growing weariness, replenishing their emotional banks from numerous small victories here and there. Women were distinguishing themselves in all sectors of society: Clara Barton, the Civil War's "Angel of the Battlefield," founded the American Red Cross and Belva Lockwood became the first woman attorney to argue a case before the Supreme Court -- to name just two. Partial suffrage was gained in several states for local elections. And the ever-increasing number of university-trained women was demonstrating the intellectual equality of the sexes.

At the national level, things fared no better. Susan B. Anthony found a helpful ally in California Senator A.A. Sargent. At Anthony's urging, he introduced a woman suffrage amendment in 1878, which was ridiculed and promptly defeated. Known eventually as the "Susan B. Anthony amendment," it was reintroduced by Sargent session after session, and routinely defeated. Anthony and her forces delivered millions of petitions to Congress and even tried using pretty, young suffragettes to testify, to no avail.

Unfortunately, bigotry in the political world joined the resistance in the liquor industry and the conservative religious community. Congressmen from the South found the very notion of enfranchising black women revolting and northern representatives rejected the notion of giving the vote to immigrant women, who were increasingly Catholic and Jewish. It was not one of Congress' finest hours.

There was, somewhat unexpectedly, progress at the international level. The suffrage movement in the United States was far ahead of any comparable movement in any other country in the world -- in spite of its inch-by-inch progress -- and our leaders were held in awe by European wannabes. In 1878, the first International Woman's Rights Congress was held coincidental with an international trade exposition in Paris. In a rare show of unity, Stanton, Anthony, Stone and Howe attended and worked together with representatives from most major European countries. Howe was elected co-president. In a follow-up meeting in London in 1883, Stanton and Anthony were honored for their leadership, and the Big One was planned for Washington, D.C. in 1888.

A whopping 49 countries were represented at the Washington convocation. Eight days of proceedings touched on every dimension of women's rights. And a permanent body, the International Council of Women, was created. Paradoxically, the conference was expressly intended to celebrate the 40th anniversary of the by-then internationally famous Seneca Falls convention but, unlike it, the attending nations' representatives felt asking for the vote was going too far. Indeed, the attending nations had much catching up to do.

But the odds were stacked in their favor. Most European nations were racially, culturally and religiously homogeneous. They lacked sizable minorities that the majority feared to enfranchise. Unlike the U.S., they were accustomed to large, central governments -- monarchies or the democracies that replaced them; therefore, there was no need to split forces between a "bottom-up" (state) or a "top-down" (national) strategy. The road ahead of those European nations contained fewer potholes than in the U.S.

The Gay Nineties

The wheel-spinning experiences of 1870-1890 were discouraging and the aging leaders began to wonder whether the grim reaper would arrive before victory. A few events in the 1890s, however, did suggest that the tide was beginning to turn.

The daughters of Lucy Stone and Elizabeth Stanton had grown to adulthood during the struggle, embraced the suffrage cause themselves and found they enjoyed working together. They convinced their mothers to put old differences aside in the interest of unity. Accordingly the National WSA and the American WSA merged in 1890 into the National American WSA. Stanton was its first president, Anthony thereafter. Stone, in failing health, basically allowed the National WSA to absorb her organization; she would deliver her last speech at the 1893 Columbian Exposition in Chicago.

South Dakota provided the first test for the new organization, with the same old results. Woman suffrage received only one-third of the vote whereas Indian suffrage received nearly 50%. It was one more slap in the face: the male establishment would rather give the vote to non-taxpaying Indian men than to taxpaying females.

In 1893, however, an unexpected victory jolted the woman suffrage movement both here and abroad. **New Zealand, of all places, became the first country in the world to fully enfranchise its women!** It did so on its own, like Wyoming and Utah, without any outside influence or assistance. Suffragettes around the world rejoiced in this unexpected prize, but were also a little confused about its importance internationally. It quite definitely was a victory, but not in a trend-setting country.

In the same year, however, Colorado fully enfranchised its women and Idaho did likewise in 1896. With Wyoming attaining statehood in 1890 and Utah in 1896, suddenly the country had full woman suffrage in four states, all in the West!

The campaigns in Colorado and Utah differed markedly from the earlier, unsuccessful state campaigns. They were managed for the National American WSA by Carrie Catt, a westerner herself. They were grassroots campaigns rather than campaigns dominated by big-name suffragettes from the East: westerners were becoming disenchanted with the same old eastern ladies who told them what to do without being successful in their own states back home. The Colorado campaign emphasized having as many women as possible make personal pitches to the milkman, the policeman, the butcher, the mailman and anyone and everyone they came into contact with. Catt's campaigns also formally separated the suffrage issue from the temperance issue, and it worked!

Meanwhile, ever-increasing numbers of women marched to college, took responsible positions in the labor force and joined everything in sight. Enterprising, self-sufficient, capable women were no longer novelties.

At the international level, the movement expanded significantly at the 1893 Columbian exposition in Chicago. There, 330 speakers addressed 150,000 women from 27 countries; the proceedings filled six volumes. Interestingly, representatives from other countries had worked through their earlier fear of setting woman suffrage as a goal.

Perhaps most importantly of all, social order didn't collapse in the states with full or partial woman suffrage.

After Wyoming enfranchised its women, for example, they were required to fulfill the duties of registered voters, such as serving on juries. When the first women were called to jury duty there, the national press that had ignored their enfranchisement ridiculed that dumbing of the judicial system. But the women conducted themselves admirably and the nay-sayers were forced to seek other targets for their venom.

Similarly, nearly two dozen states had granted partial suffrage to women, most often for local school elections. Nothing scandalous resulted. The schools didn't collapse. Life went on.

Somehow, society seemed to be surviving the coming out of its better half. Surprise, surprise.

Father Time Catches up

By 1900, the first generation's suffragettes were either dead or close to it and the two main second generation leaders for the 20th century (Carrie Catt and Alice Paul) were revving up. The two generations' leaders shared one characteristic: they all lived longer than their contemporaries. Only Lucy Stone died in her seventies; Sojourner Truth, Lucretia Mott, Elizabeth Cady Stanton and Susan B. Anthony all died in their late eighties; Julia Ward Howe and Alice Paul passed away in their nineties.

Lucretia Mott (1880) and Sojourner Truth (1883) died first after years of declining activity. Lucy Stone similarly reduced her workload before her 1893 death, but she took one final, posthumous shot at convention: she had her remains cremated, an infrequent and religiously unpopular practice at the time.

Stanton's excessive weight and failing eyesight constrained her physical mobility for the last decade of her life, but not her pen. She could have spent her final years accepting one honor after another both in the U.S. and around the world, but there was one more societal wound she wanted to rub salt into. In 1895, she published her next-to-last book, *The Woman's Bible*, in which she refuted the submissive status of women that conservatives propounded from scripture. It was a bombshell out of the blue.

Members of the National American WSA reacted with shock and anger. Since the early hostility from the religious community had mellowed a little, most suffragettes wanted to let sleeping dogs lie. They had their hands full with racism in the South, bigotry in the North and foes of prohibition everywhere. Why stir up the conservative religious community?

Members of the National American WSA introduced this resolution at their 1896 convention: " . . . that this Association is non-sectarian and it has no connection with the so-called *Woman's Bible* or any other theological publication."

Susan B. Anthony left the chair to speak against the resolution, reminding the members that Stanton had founded the movement and led it for an entire half-century. Unconvinced, the members passed the resolution easily. Stanton, deeply hurt, withdrew from active participation in the organization. The woman suffrage movement had become conservative with a single plank in its women's rights platform. Stanton's funeral in 1902 was attended by a small number of friends and relatives, a sad farewell to one of the most influential women in American history, if not THE most influential.

Susan B. Anthony alone continued her leadership role with seemingly unlimited energy up to her death in 1906. When Stanton asked her to withdraw from the National American WSA after Stanton's censure, Susan was in agony for weeks. Torn between her half-century friendship with Stanton and her devotion to the cause, she finally decided the cause took precedence, and stayed. The relationship between the two leaders survived the ordeal and Anthony visited her failing friend many times before her 1902 death.

Anthony, the lonely survivor from the early days with no family of her own and few living friends, survived Stanton by four years. If anyone truly was married to her work, it was Anthony, active and influential to the very end and the beloved symbol of all that was right in the women's rights movement. Two years before her death in 1906, she traveled all the way to Germany for a conference. And just months before her death, she delivered a major address in Baltimore.

Although Anthony always credited Stanton with founding the women's rights movement, it was she who pulled suffrage out of Stanton's broader agenda and fought for it decade after decade, in Congress and in the states, in conference after conference, meeting after endless meetings, here and abroad. The U.S. government later honored her on two stamps and one dollar coin. "Awesome" understates her commitment.

Julia Ward Howe was the last to die -- in 1910 at 91 years of age. And her departure was as extravagant as Stanton's had been humble. At her memorial service in Boston's Symphony Hall, a choir four-thousand strong sang her *Battle Hymn of the Republic.* Her eyes had truly seen the glory . . . .

Lucretia Mott, Elizabeth Cady Stanton, Lucy Stone, Sojourner Truth, Julia Ward Howe -- they had taken an idea, an unpopular idea, and moved it toward reality for an entire half of the U.S. population, inspiring countless others to leadership both here and around the world.

Seventy-two years passed from the revolutionary ideals in the Declaration of Independence to the revolutionary ideals in the Seneca Falls convention, and it would take seventy-two more years for woman suffrage to become the law of the land. It was the longest battle in U.S. history, and it required a second generation of leaders to bring it to conclusion.

Chapter Appendix
The Woman's Bible

Only Elizabeth Cady Stanton ended her women's rights career with less than the unrestrained affection of her colleagues and followers. Her book, *The Woman's Bible.* touched such a raw nerve in female society that the suffragettes in the very organization she founded and led for decades voted to disassociate themselves from it and her, in effect censuring her. Deeply hurt, she disassociated herself from them, leaving Susan B. Anthony to continue the movement. It was an unfortunate experience that merits an analysis of how and why it occurred.

First, what was *The Woman's Bible*?

It actually was two volumes, the first published in 1895 and the second in 1898. Since the National American Woman Suffrage Association disassociated itself from *The Woman Bible* in 1896, it did so only in reaction to the first volume, which was the lesser of the two, covering the first five books of the Bible. The second volume covered the remainder of the Old Testament and the entire New Testament.

Stanton and a revising committee literally cut out over 150 short passages from the Bible that had anything to do with women -- over 70 percent were from the Old Testament -- and Stanton and/or one of her colleagues wrote a short commentary on each one. The majority of the passages and commentaries were historical in nature, not controversial. If persons had read only the passages and commentaries, there would have been no organized reaction.

The problem arose because Stanton introduced the first volume with a scathing attack on theology, the Bible and the entire Christian tradition. It was a diplomatic *faux pas* of the first order. Here are three paragraphs from page one of a seven-page introduction.

> **From the inauguration of the movement for woman's emancipation the Bible has been used to hold her in the "divinely ordained sphere" prescribed in the Old and New Testaments. The canon and civil law; church and state; priests and legislators; all political parties and religious denominations have alike taught that woman was made after man, of man, and for man, an inferior being, subject to man. Creeds, codes, scriptures, and statutes, are all based on this idea. The fashions, forms, ceremonies and customs of society, church ordinances and discipline all grow out of this idea.**
>
> **The Bible teaches that woman brought sin and death into the world, that she precipitated the fall of the race, that she was arraigned before the judgment seat of Heaven, tried, condemned and sentenced. Marriage to her was to be a condition of bondage, maternity a period of suffering and anguish, and in silence and subjection, she was to play the role of a dependent on man's bounty for all her material wants, and for all the information she might desire on the vital questions of the hour, she was commanded to ask her husband at home.**

With such an explosive preamble, it is doubtful that many of the religiously sensitive suffragettes read much of the remainder of the first volume or any of the second. That is unfortunate because the second volume contains an entirely different attitude toward the teaching of Christ. For instance, the following passage (pp. 164-165):

> **Jesus is not recorded as having uttered any similar claim that a woman should be subject to a man, or that in teaching she would be a usurper. The dominion of woman over man or of man over woman makes no part of the sayings of the Nazarene. He spoke to the individual soul, not recognizing sex as a quality of spiritual life, or as determining the sphere of action of either man or woman.**

Having thus ingratiated herself to the religiously sensitive in the second volume, however, Stanton concludes that volume with another salvo:

> **The real difficulty in woman's case is that the whole foundation of the Christian religion rests on her temptation and man's fall, hence the necessity of a Redeemer and a plan of salvation. As the chief cause of this dire calamity, woman's degradation and subordination were made a necessity. If, however, we accept the Darwinian theory, that the race has been a gradual growth from the lower to a higher form of life, and that the story of the fall is a myth, we can exonerate the snake, emancipate the woman, and reconstruct a more rational religion for the nineteenth century, and thus escape all the perplexities of the Jewish mythology as of no more importance that those of the Greek, Persian and Egyptian.**

Without question, no one ever accused Stanton of being conventional, shy, inarticulate or indecisive. What she thought was what she wrote -- unfiltered.

Just how did Stanton come to deviate so far from the dogma of the day and from the prevailing beliefs of her sisters in the cause?

Elizabeth Cady was born into a conservative Presbyterian family dominated by her stern, lawyer/judge father. Her autobiography, filled with references to her father, rarely mentions her mother.

Elizabeth's older brother died when she was eleven. She seems to have been more distressed by her father's grief response than by the boy's death. When she climbed on his knee to comfort him, he responded, "Oh, you should have been a boy."

At a tender age, therefore, Elizabeth was introduced to the notion, strange and repellent to her, that she was somehow less a person because of her gender. Her father's law practice reinforced that notion. His office adjoined the house and there usually were several law students there. From Stanton's autobiography (pp. 31-32):

> ... I spent much of my time (at my father's office), listening to the clients stating their cases, talking with the students, and reading the laws in regard to woman. . . . The tears and complaints of the women who came to my father for legal advice touched my heart and early drew my attention to the injustice and cruelty of the laws. As the practice of the law was my father's business, I could not exactly understand why he could not alleviate the sufferings of these women. So, in order to enlighten me, he would take down

his books and show me the inexorable statutes. The students, observing my interest, would amuse themselves by reading to me all the worst laws they could find, over which I would laugh and cry by turns. One Christmas morning I went into the office to show them, among other of my presents, a new coral necklace and bracelets. They all admired the jewelry and then began to tease me with hypothetical cases of future ownership. "Now," said Henry Bayard, "if in due time you should be my wife, those ornaments would be mine; I could take them and lock them up, and you could never wear them except with my permission. I could even exchange them for a box of cigars, and you could watch them evaporate in smoke."

The bantering with the law students obviously educated Elizabeth in the law, sharpened her wit, taught her that legality and justice were not always the same, and introduced her to the adversarial, confrontational style that would characterize her later years. It was a unique education on which she built her life.

Although young Elizabeth formed a close relationship with her Presbyterian minister, she recalls in her autobiography an early aversion to religion which seemed to her so gloomy and based on fear. She found the law students' books much more to her liking.

Of all the women without redress under the law, Elizabeth seems to have sympathized most completely with those trapped in abusive marriages to drunken husbands. In her young mind, such entrapment was completely and inexcusably wrong. Any person or law or dogma or custom that contributed to it was evil, wrong, debasing and legion other adjectives. And it was this conclusion that helped her develop the broadest perspective on women's rights in her time.

To escape from grotesque marriages, women would need new laws that would allow her to sue in court and more liberal grounds for divorce. Since they could take no wealth or children with them, new laws were needed on property rights and child custody. Outside the legal sphere, they needed equal educational and vocational opportunities if they were to support themselves, and equal pay for equal work. Male clergy must cease advising them to remain in the marriage no matter how atrocious life became. And women needed equal access to the pulpit and the ballot box to help redress the grievances and injustices all women experienced. In short, without total equality in everything, no one reform would amount to much. *That* was Elizabeth Cady Stanton and that was her life. Total equality and nothing less. It was radical reform that would affect one-half of the population.

It was a vision not shared by the religious and civil communities, whose perceptions of the subordinate female had grown together over the centuries. Even mild deviations from the norm of submission drew flak from male clergy. Even when women ventured out into the community in auxiliaries supporting temperance and abolition movements run by men, ministerial eyebrows were raised even though most ministers supported both movements; the following is from a 1837 pastoral letter sent to all the clergymen in New England (*History of Woman Suffrage*, Vol. 1, p. 81):

> **We invite your attention to the dangers which at present seem to threaten the female character with wide-spread and permanent injury. The appropriate duties and influences of woman are clearly stated in the New Testament . . . . The power of woman is her dependence, flowing from**

the consciousness of that weakness God has given her for her protection.

We appreciate the unostentatious prayers and efforts of woman in advancing the cause of religion at home and abroad . . . . But when she assumes the place and tone of man as a public reformer, our care and protection of her seem unnecessary; we put ourselves in self-defence against her; she yields the power God has given her for her protection, and her character becomes unnatural . . . . We can not, therefore, but regret the mistaken conduct of those who encourage females to bear an obtrusive and ostentatious part in measures of reform, and countenance any of that sex who so far forget themselves as to itinerate in the character of public lecturers and teachers.

It was a harbinger of the male-controlled, Christian community's response to women who would seek equality in any manner, shape or form.

By the time of Elizabeth's 1840 wedding, she had rejected anything that obstructed total equality for women and had heard the backlash from outraged ministers. Undeterred, she and her husband deleted the word, obey, from their marriage vows, unaware that this scandalous act would gain instant and widespread notoriety for both of them.

The Stantons' honeymoon in London exposed Elizabeth to two more defining experiences. There she met Lucretia Mott, a Quaker minister in the Hicksite sect, whose vision of sexual equality energized Elizabeth, but Mott was considered a dangerous woman in her larger denomination. And American clergy participated in the exclusion of women from the World Anti-Slavery Convention. Thus, there were splits and tensions within and between religious and reform organizations. Seemingly no move by anyone in any direction would go unchecked by someone or some body.

Eight years later, at the world-shaking Seneca Falls convention, the female participants wanted *into* the inner sanctums of their churches, not out of them, and were shocked at the ridicule of the idea from the nation's pulpits.

Lucy Stone had been excommunicated for questioning some translations of Biblical passages and ministers ganged up against women's rights conventions, such as the one mentioned earlier in Akron, Ohio.

The early philosophy of the women's rights movement drew heavily on the country's religious tradition and the Declaration of Independence's citation of God-given inalienable rights. Such a strategy seemed questionable, however, without the support of the clergy. Given that, Ernestine Rose became the first to formally divorce her reform philosophy from Scripture. She did so in response to the Rev. Antoinnette L. Brown who had made a valiant, but unconvincing, argument that the woman's cause and the Bible were compatible (*History of Woman Suffrage*, Vol. 1., pp. 536-537):

> For my part, I see no need to appeal to any written authority, particularly when it is so obscure and indefinite as to admit to different interpretations. When the inhabitants of Boston converted their harbor into a teapot rather than submit to unjust taxes, they did not go to the Bible for their authority; for if they had, they would have been told from the same authority to "give unto Caesar what belonged to Caesar" ... No! on Human Rights and Freedom, on a subject

that is as self-evident as that two and two make
four, there is no need of any written authority.

Resolved, That we ask not for our rights as a gift
of charity, but as an act of justice. . . . And any
difference . . . in political, civil and social rights,
on account of sex, is in direct violation of the
principles of justice and humanity, and as such
ought to be held up to the contempt and derision
of every lover of human freedom.

Elizabeth Cady Stanton also began to separate her
arguments from traditional Christianity. In 1853 she
addressed a women's temperance society and unveiled her
emerging concern about the authority that hostile
clergymen cited against women reformers -- the Bible
(*History of Woman Suffrage,* Vol. 1, pp. 496-497):

But why attack the church? We do not attack
the Church; we defend ourselves merely against
its attacks . . . . Reformers on all sides claim for
themselves a higher position than the Church.
Our God is a God of justice, mercy and truth.
Their God sanctions violence, oppression, and
wine-bibbing, and winks at gross moral
delinquencies. Our Bible commands us to love
our enemies; to resist not evil; to break every
yoke and let the oppressed go free; and makes a
noble life of more importance than a stern faith.
Their Bible permits war, slavery, capital
punishment, and makes salvation depend on
faith and ordinances . . . .

All of our reformers have, in a measure, been
developed in the Church, and all our reforms
have started there. The advocates and opposers
of the reforms of our day, have grown up side by
side, partaking of the same ordinances and

officiating at the same altars; but one, by applying more fully his Christian principles to life, and pursuing an admitted truth to its legitimate results, has unwittingly found himself in antagonism with his brother.

Thus, Stanton clearly states her belief that the clergy had cast the first stone in the early clashes between female reformers and traditional clergy; the reformers were forced to defend themselves. Furthermore, traditional Christianity sported a double standard -- one standard for ideals and another for practice. It was the practice the reformers were attempting to change. In 1853, it seems, Stanton had one foot in the Christian community and one foot out, a compromising position that could not last indefinitely.

As the years passed, Stanton came more and more to believe the Bible was the ultimate source of trouble, or at least its interpretation. Several clergymen had come to the defense of the feminists, proving that Christian dogma and women's rights were not incompatible in the eyes of all clergymen. But it was the Bible that hostile clergy always cited -- from Eve's cause of the Fall in Genesis to Paul's dictum to women to shut up, sit down and wear a hat in church, and dozens of passages in-between.

Then, as now, scholars disagreed on the very nature of the Bible. At one extreme, God was considered its author and every word was to be taken as His will. At the other, it was considered a loose collection of historical recollections by men whose very identity was subject to debate. The more radical feminists, including Stanton, leaned toward the latter view which allowed them to attribute women's inferior status to the customs of the writers' times, not to Divine mandate.

Although the Civil War and the preoccupation with suffrage after it moved the religious issue to the background, it was Stanton whose persistence kept it alive by introducing resolutions at annual conventions, which were routinely watered-down. One in 1885, a decade before the publication of *The Woman's Bible*, is particularly revealing (excerpt from autobiography, p. 381)).

> **WHEREAS, The dogmas incorporated in religious creeds derived from Judaism, teaching that woman was an after-thought in the creation, her sex a misfortune, marriage a condition of subordination, and maternity a curse, are contrary to the law of God (as revealed in nature), and to the precepts of Christ . . . .**

Stanton rejoiced in the strong reaction from suffragettes to this *relatively* mild resolution. Her associates had changed her wording to pin some of the blame on Jews, which drew an angry (and justified, in Stanton's opinion) reaction from Jewish feminists. Additionally, the publication of the resolution in the nation's newspapers drew fire from pulpits everywhere. The response from Rev. Patton of Howard University was so vitriolic toward women in general that even his own non-feminist parishioners rebuked him and he refused to share his sermon notes for *verbatim* quotation in the press.

Stanton summarized her response as follows (autobiography, p. 383).

> **Women are now making their attacks on the Church all along the line. They are demanding their right to be ordained as ministers, elders, deacons, and to be received as delegates in all the ecclesiastical convocations. At last they ask of the Church just what they have asked of the State for the last half-century -- perfect equality -- and the clergy, as a body, are quite as hostile to their demands as the statesmen.**

Stanton does candidly admit in this passage that she had frontally attacked the Church, but she also states clearly that the attack was a means to an end rather than an end unto itself. The end or goal was equality for women *within* religion, not the destruction of religion. It was her failure to make that distinction in *The Woman's Bible* that cost her so dearly.

Carrie Chapman Catt, who led the suffragettes to victory in the post-Stanton/Anthony era, was an early member of Stanton's revising committee for *The Woman's Bible,* but distanced herself from its preparation when she got the gist of Stanton's intentions. Interestingly, her views generally resembled Stanton's. From her 1924 history of the suffrage movement (p. 4):

> **Neither the man movement nor the woman movement had a dated beginning. In the struggle upward toward political freedom, men were called upon to overthrow the universally accepted theory of the Divine Right of Kings to rule over the masses of men; women, the universally accepted theory of the Divine Right of Men to rule over women. The American Revolution forever destroyed the Divine Right of Kings theory in this country but left untouched the theory of the Divine Right of Man to rule over woman. Men and women believed it with equal sincerity, the church taught it, customs were based upon it, the law endorsed it, and the causes that created the belief had been so long lost in obscurity that men claimed authority for it in the "laws of God." All opposition to the enfranchisement of women emanated from that theory.**

In spite of sharing Stanton's conviction that the Church had contributed for centuries to women's subordination, she voted with those favoring a censure of Stanton. Given her belief that woman suffrage could be attained only through a massive populist lobby on its behalf, what purpose would a controversial book serve if it alienated a large body of supporters?

Others in the suffrage movement agreed with her and shared her single-plank dedication. Whereas Stanton wanted equality for women in everything, not just suffrage, and worked toward all goals all the time, Catt as a superior strategist recognized the wisdom of pursuing one goal at a time. And suffrage was her goal.

Similarly, other suffragettes reacted negatively to Stanton's book because their pursuit of enfranchisement did not compromise their religious beliefs. Indeed, suffrage was the least religiously controversial of all the woman's rights goals. Voting was a secular function, not religious, and took virtually no time away from the family; clergy were (and still are) concerned that emancipated women would compromise the quality of family life in their pursuit of meaningful activities outside the home. So many suffragettes held this and similar views that the movement as a whole had become conservative, and Stanton's more radical views made very unwelcome waves.

Appreciative as the burgeoning suffrage membership was of Stanton's pioneering efforts over the decades, times had changed and the cause's membership had changed and that membership wanted Stanton muzzled, which it did. It was not a happy occasion for anyone.

In 1848, woman suffrage seemed the most elusive goal. As it has turned out, religious equality really was and still is and will be until consensus is reached on the interpretation of the Bible, if ever. Only Stanton foresaw that.

However, Elizabeth did not foresee that the Presbyterian denomination of her childhood would become a mid-twentieth century leader in ordaining women. More than that, Presbyterian scholars in the new millennium would write the very observations and convictions for which she had been vilified (e.g., the following excerpts from pp. 141-145 by Jack Rogers, a seminary professor, Year 2000).

> **As with slavery, Presbyterians in the nineteenth century defended the status quo that prohibited women, among other things, from voting or owning property. Men selected proof texts from the Bible that described the cultural role of women in the ancient Near Eastern culture and used them to justify their own subordination of women. We forget how passionately leading Presbyterian theologians felt they were defending the Bible by rejecting women's rights. . . We said women were not rational and were unprepared for public life in order to deny them access to education and restrict their service to homemaking and child care. We justified these cultural prejudices in the name of God and on the basis of the Bible. . . . We should be sobered by how wrong we were for so long regarding African Americans and women.**

If alive today, Stanton might find it ironic that, at least in one Christian denomination, some nineteenth century heresies have become twenty-first century dogma.

Chapter 7

The Agony and the Ecstasy

During the last half of the nineteenth century, Elizabeth Cady Stanton and Lucy Stone began as allies with an agenda that, at first, included suffrage as just a minor plank in a broad women's rights platform. After a cordial working relationship of nearly 20 years, they parted company into rival organizations, each with suffrage as its highest priority, but with different strategies.

As the first generation of suffrage leaders died off, they were replaced by two twentieth century leaders who also began as co-workers, but ended as heads of competing organizations with different strategies. Carrie Catt and Alice Paul, as it turned out, implemented rival strategies that actually ended up complementing each other.

Carrie Lane Chapman Catt (1859-1947)

Carrie Catt proved to be the most versatile of all the suffrage leaders. She wrote as well as Stanton, possessed Anthony's energy and organizational genius, was college-educated like Stone, and shared the dedication and leadership qualities of all her predecessors.

Carrie Lane was born in 1859 into a Wisconsin farm family that moved to Iowa when she was seven. After an uneventful childhood, her father, like Stone's, refused to finance a full college education, so she worked her way through Iowa State Agricultural College.

In rapid succession, Carrie Lane graduated from college, read law for a short period, became a high school principal (unusual for a woman then), became a superintendent of schools (remarkable then), married Leo Chapman, helped him edit his newspaper, traveled to California to join him after he had moved earlier to set up his business, found on arrival that he had died of typhoid fever, supported herself as a newspaper reporter, returned to Iowa and married wealthy engineer George Catt. By age 30, she had packed more living into her life than most did in a full lifetime.

Carrie's marriage to George Catt was as unique as Elizabeth Stanton's and Lucy Stone's. Elizabeth had deleted any reference to "obey" in her marriage vows and Lucy retained her maiden name, Stone. Carrie, as the story goes - - and it has been disputed -- insisted on a agreement with George that she be allowed to work on woman suffrage for two months each fall and two months each spring. She had joined the Iowa Woman Suffrage Association three years earlier (1887) and instantly recognized her life's work. It consumed her for most of the next 33 years.

Again in rapid succession, Carrie and her husband moved to New York, she attended the 1890 meeting that united the Stanton and Stone factions into the National American Woman Suffrage Association and rose quickly through the ranks to chair the Organization Committee.

Then it got interesting. Representing the national organization, Carrie ran her own brand of grassroot, bottom-up suffrage campaigns in Colorado (1893) and Idaho (1896), succeeding in both, the last states to grant full woman suffrage for the next dozen years.

By the end of the century, therefore, four contiguous western states had granted suffrage (Wyoming, Utah, Colorado and Idaho) and one country (New Zealand). By that time, the opponents of woman suffrage knew the movement wouldn't fold, and the suffragettes knew the opposition wouldn't, either. A pier five brawl was brewing.

The aging but indefatigable Susan B. Anthony led the charge into the twentieth century. Her battle cry of "victory is inevitable" apparently electrified the movement because all her contemporaries and modern writers alike quote it. The national woman suffrage amendment, submitted to Congress session after session, eventually became known as the Susan B. Anthony Amendment. Australia (1902) became the second country in the world to fully enfranchise its women and Finland (1906) followed suit. It truly was a world war. No other conflict in history had ever been fought on so many fronts.

Even Anthony was mortal, however, and she resigned as president of the National American WSA at the turn of the century. Even so, she remained active right up to her 1906 death. She was also a shrewd judge of people. She picked her successor, whom all assumed would be the Rev. Dr. Anna Howard Shaw, who had degrees in theology and medicine and was a gifted orator. Instead, Anthony picked Carrie Catt, whose organizational abilities matched her own, and Catt assumed the presidency in 1900.

It proved to be a short term in office with no impressive victories. State after state defeated suffrage referenda and the Susan B. Anthony amendment fared no better in

Congress. With her husband dying, Catt resigned the presidency in 1904 to care for him. Anna Shaw led the organization for the next 10 years.

"Led" is a poor choice of words. Shaw, admired for her education and liked for her personality and respected for her speaking skills, lacked the organizational talents of Anthony and Catt, and the organization gradually fell into disarray. At the same time, however, suffrage victories at the state level began to mushroom in 1910. In rapid succession, full suffrage was won in Washington (1910), California (1911), Oregon (1912), Arizona (1912), Kansas (1912), Nevada (1914) and Montana (1914). Except for New Mexico, the entire western third of the country had granted full suffrage. With many of the remaining states granting some form of local suffrage, the South remained the only completely resistant section of the country. Norway (1913) joined the trend in Europe. Finally, there seemed to be some light at the end of the tunnel.

Alice Paul (1885-1977)

Alice Paul joined the U.S. suffrage movement in her mid-twenties, less than a decade before the nineteenth Amendment gave full suffrage to all women in all states. In that time, short in comparison to the other major suffrage leaders, she equaled their contribution to the cause by introducing militant methods to a stagnant movement.

Alice was born in 1885 into an affluent, liberal Quaker family in New Jersey. She graduated from Swarthmore College in 1905 and took her master's from the University of Pennsylvania in 1907. For the next three years, Paul did graduate work, especially in England.

Elizabeth Cady Stanton had been considered a radical in nineteenth century America but would have been deemed moderate in twentieth century England. There, the suffrage organizations emphasized visibility at all cost and pressure tactics of all sorts. During Alice Paul's stay there, she learned to demonstrate, parade and picket. With her English sisters, she was jailed occasionally and was even forcibly tube-fed during hunger strikes. She witnessed hyper-committed suffragettes willing to stop at nothing, including destruction of property and harassment of officials. (The term, suffragette, was coined in England to characterize militant female suffragists, but did not carry that type of connotation in the U.S.)

Returning to the U.S. in 1910 and attending a NAWSA convention, Alice was appalled at the pervasive conservatism in the organization as led by Anna Shaw. Although she was preoccupied with her Ph.D. program until 1912, she was active in NAWSA but found a kindred soul outside it in Harriet Stanton Blatch.

Harriet, the daughter of Elizabeth Cady Stanton, had lived in England with her husband and child until returning to the U.S. in 1902. Like Paul later, Blatch was astonished at the conservatism in her mother's organization and, like Paul, developed a distinct preference for English militant methods. She founded the Equality League of Self-Supporting Women, a body of working class women whom the middle class NAWSA had shunned. By 1912, membership had grown to 20,000.

That was a presidential election year and, after Woodrow Wilson's victory, Blatch and her followers marched from New York City to Albany, the state capital, to lobby for suffrage. It took 13 days in bitter cold, which drew throngs of sympathetic reporters. Encouraged by their published accounts, Blatch and her hardy supporters trudged the 250 miles to the nation's capital for Wilson's 1913 inauguration. (At that time, inaugurations were held in March.) There she joined ranks with Alice Paul.

Paul had organized a parade for the day before the inauguration. About 8,000 white-clad women tramped along the city's streets, proudly proclaiming their dedication to the cause. Unfortunately, groups of half-soused bullies roughed up the marchers to the dismay of all sensible persons. Again, newspaper accounts across the country praised the suffragettes. The police chief was fired for his ineptness.

Encouraged by the parade and the public's sympathy with it, Paul immediately created the Congressional Union (CU) within the NAWSA and surrounded herself with young, educated, aggressive women. They opened an office in D.C., offered training courses, sponsored parades and demonstrations, submitted petitions to Congress and generally left the stagnant NAWSA in their wake.

Refreshing as CU's burst of energy was, it soon alienated the larger NAWSA leadership. Paul was convinced that the aggressive English model should replace the staid, old-fashioned NAWSA model of education and negotiation that had ground the organization almost to a standstill. Polite requests for woman suffrage had failed decade after decade. In contrast, the English model featured visibility in the forms of parades, pickets and demonstrations. But it also featured attacking the party in power in an attempt to bludgeon it into submission.

That tactic was well-suited to British government. The prime minister was elected by Parliament, not the people, which provided a uniform party majority for the legislative and executive functions of government. In the U.S., however, the president's party may differ from the parties in power in Congress. In theory, at least, the president may favor woman suffrage but the controlling parties in Congress may not. Attacking the president's party, therefore, would be counterproductive.

There was some support for woman suffrage in both the Republican and Democratic parties, and President Wilson, taking office in 1913, was leaning more toward support than any previous president. Working against the party in power, therefore, threatened to alienate a promising president and reduce the number of supporters in his party in both houses of Congress. The leadership of NAWSA viewed that as total insanity and sought to constrain Paul's loose canon in the organization.

Alice responded by withdrawing her Congressional Union from NAWSA in 1914 and then also creating a new organization, the National Women's Party, in 1916. (The term, party, is misleading because the new program never sponsored anyone for office.) In the 1914 Congressional elections, the CU helped defeat 20 Democrats who supported suffrage. Paul hoped the lost support from them would be outweighed by more responsive Congressmen who wanted to keep their seats in the next election.

Paul's defection from NAWSA was only the last of many during Anna Shaw's presidency. In failing health, Shaw got the message and announced her retirement. Thus in 1915 Carrie Catt was elected to succeed her in 1916.

The times were quite different from Carrie's first stint in office. President Wilson was up for reelection. Prohibition organizations were steadily gaining the upper hand in a life-and-death struggle with the liquor industry. World War I, which began in Europe in 1914, threatened to draw the U.S. into the fray. Contraception was becoming one of the more explosive issues of the day with obvious implications for women's rights. Indeed, Catt returned to office in a highly energized atmosphere.

At least the rest of the world was making progress with woman suffrage, especially in Europe. Including countries mentioned above, here is a partial list of major nations granting woman suffrage to 1920.

1893 - New Zealand
1902 - Australia
1906 - Finland
1913 - Norway
1915 - Denmark
1917 - Soviet Union
1918 - Canada
1920 - Austria
1920 - Germany
1920 - Poland
1920 - Sweden

Carrie Catt estimated that 26 nations, large and small, beat the U.S. to woman suffrage or tied it, a not too exemplary record for a country that prided itself on being the world's leader in democracy. Yet the successes in other countries gave her confidence that the U.S. would convert, and *soon.*

Illinois: the Turning Point

Before Catt assumed NAWSA's presidency, the long-suffering suffrage movement finally turned the corner in 1913 in an unlikely state: Illinois. Buffering the eastern and western halves of the country, it was surrounded by non-suffrage states and it innovated in a way that dominoed through them.

Partial suffrage had enjoyed limited success in states earlier in the form of municipal elections or specialty elections, such as for school board membership. An adverse Supreme Court decision in 1893 on municipal suffrage in Michigan, however, brought that form of partial suffrage to a virtual standstill. But in 1913, suffragists sensed a favorable attitude in Illinois. To test it, female suffrage attorneys introduced a bill in the state legislature for both municipal and presidential suffrage.

Presidential suffrage was an untried form of partial suffrage that had been a gleam in the suffrage eye for decades. Since persons were citizens of both states and the nation, separate decisions seemed justified on who could vote in each. Since the Supreme Court had vested such decisions in the states and since granting women the presidential vote did not compromise the control of state affairs by state party bosses, those politicians found presidential (partial) suffrage a relatively small pill to swallow. Indeed, tossing an appeasing bone to the suffragettes might take some heat off them, at least for a while. No state (except for an anemic attempt in Rhode Island) had bothered to legalize presidential suffrage for women because no one knew whether it would pass the inevitable Supreme Court test.

Finally, however, Illinois tried and, lo and behold, the bill passed in spite of vitriolic lobbying by the liquor industry and general male antipathy. Lo and behold again, it survived both a Supreme Court test in 1914 and a state repeal effort by the anti-suffrage forces.

The significance of the victory became crystal clear at the next state elections. Over 250,000 gleeful women voted in Chicago, the nation's second largest city at the time, thereby obliterating the antis' argument that women didn't really want the vote. Statewide, according to newspaper reports, over a thousand saloons had been closed by the vote. Both male and female prohibitionists, an organized army in the millions, previously had distanced themselves from the suffrage movement, which they had seen as a go-nowhere movement. But the Illinois vote changed that and brought countless prohibitionists to the cause.

Jubilant suffrage leaders immediately put the Illinois experience into national context. The first four states to grant woman suffrage controlled only 17 Electoral College votes for electing the nation's president. Washington and California added 20 more. All the other western states with suffrage -- all with small populations -- added only 18 more. Heavily populated Illinois, however, added 29 all by itself. Suffrage states were beginning to wield some political muscle.

Adding additional populous states with presidential suffrage would obviously give females even more clout. More than that, it meant that politicians at the national level had to court the female vote to put their party in the White House, even if they represented states with no form of suffrage at all. That, in turn, would expand Congressional support for a Constitutional amendment. And that, in turn, would require full suffrage everywhere, even in states that had granted only presidential suffrage to placate the noisy feminist lobby. In short, state politicians who supported presidential suffrage for short-term relief were actually supporting full suffrage in the long run. Shot themselves in the foot, actually.

Catt understood the large picture fully and built into it her two-theatre winning plan -- state and national, simultaneously. Presidential suffrage in non-suffrage states became an immediate, top priority goal, even before Catt assumed NAWSA's presidency. And it succeeded. In short order, the Illinois breakthrough rippled out to Indiana, Iowa, Minnesota, Nebraska, North Dakota and Ohio. This tier of north-central states linked East with West, and the more distant states of Tennessee and Maine quickly brought to 11 the number of states with presidential suffrage. The female vole was incontrovertibly and irreversibly a major factor in national elections! Oh, how sweet it was.

The Odd Triangle

Carrie Catt was elected president of NAWSA during the spread of presidential suffrage and took office during President Wilson's 1916 campaign for re-election. She unveiled a five-year plan to win woman suffrage for the whole country. Although the ultimate goal in her plan was a constitutional amendment for universal woman suffrage, it called for immediate state-level activism to generate grassroot pressure on, and support in, Congress. As it turned out her plan worked perfectly.

Catt carefully avoided any diversion that would compromise her plan. A supporter of peace at nearly any cost prior to the U.S. entry into World War I, she suppressed her convictions and supported the war effort after entry. And she rejected overtures from Margaret Sanger, founder of the Planned Parenthood Association, to embrace the embryonic, controversial birth control movement. Catt was totally committed to woman suffrage and simply would not be side-tracked. So sure of victory was she that she founded the League of Women Voters before suffrage was won to prepare women to use their ballots judiciously once they got the vote.

Woodrow Wilson began his first term in 1913 with a favorable attitude toward woman suffrage, but also with a reluctance to compromise his political career by actively supporting it. His highest initial priority was keeping the country out of the war. His commitment to woman suffrage gradually increased as state-level suffrage victories continued, just as Catt had planned. He spoke favorably at suffrage conventions at Carrie Catt's invitation and received her frequently at the White House.

Alice Paul preferred to force Congress and Wilson into action rather than meekly negotiate them into support, not to say that Catt was meek, for she was anything but. Paul's parade before his 1913 first inauguration was only the first of many highly visible demonstrations. Her following had billowed into the tens of thousands. Although that number paled in comparison to Catt's two million followers, Paul's legions were more visible and more highly energized. Her pickets outside the White House became part of the Washington landscape. While Catt sipped tea with Wilson in the White House, Paul and her supporters screamed for his scalp outside. It was, indeed, an odd triangle - Catt, Paul and Wilson.

The reluctant U.S. entry into World War I in 1917 changed everything. When President Wilson ran for re-election in 1916 before entering the war, his banners read "Vote for Wilson, he kept us out of war." Alice Paul, attacking him and the entire Democratic Party, countered with "Vote against Wilson, he kept us out of Suffrage." And when the U.S. entered the war, Wilson claimed he was keeping the world safe for democracy. Paul and her legions countered with "Democracy should begin at home."

Whereas the suffragettes of the nineteenth century had suspended lobbying during the Civil War, both Paul and Catt intensified efforts in World War I. Both recognized that wartime breeds an atmosphere conducive to change, but post-war atmospheres typically turn conservative as weary groups adjust to peacetime conditions. Winning suffrage became a now-or-never matter for the two leaders, who otherwise disagreed on most matters.

Paul, predictably, turned up the heat more visibly. Picketing outside the White House became continuous -- 24 hours a day, every day, rain or shine. Possibly out of concern for wartime security and possibly because Paul was wearing people down, she and several others were arrested and sentenced to a Virginia workhouse/prison. Paul went on a 22-day hunger strike and was force-fed to keep her alive. Eventually the courts invalidated the arrests and convictions, whereupon Paul went straight back to the picket line to the amazement of her colleagues and with the praise of the press. At a time the public's consciousness was focused on the war, Paul's militant tactics kept reminding everyone that woman suffrage was still a very active issue.

Both Alice Paul and Carrie Catt used women's participation in the war to good advantage. Thousands of women worked overseas as nurses, physicians, ambulance drivers, translators, telephone operators and in countless other roles. Hundreds died. At home, women replaced the men fighting in Europe as factory workers, streetcar conductors, clerks, laborers - every type of job imaginable. Millions of women donated their time and money to relief agencies. Both Paul and Catt reminded everyone that such unrestrained service to country should be rewarded with suffrage. Catt was especially diligent about reminding everyone that many other countries had already done so, especially in Europe.

Meanwhile, the thirty-nine state suffrage associations that had endorsed Catt's "winning plan" experienced defeat after defeat in state referenda. Persistence paid off, however, and they finally got the big plum; populous New York, in 1917, granted full suffrage. It was a giant step forward that gave the woman suffrage movement a needed shot in the arm. Indeed, 1918 would be a pivotal year.

The Big Push

On January 9, 1918, President Wilson finally issued a formal request for a woman suffrage constitutional amendment. This came just after Congress had sent a prohibition amendment to the states for ratification. The liquor lobby was in its last throes.

The day after Wilson's request, Jeanette Rankin (D-Montana), the first woman elected to Congress, opened the House debate on the Susan B. Anthony amendment. The vote couldn't have been closer. The 274-136 tally was exactly the two-thirds majority needed for passage. Victory was in sight.

But not yet. Seven pro-suffrage senators died during the winter of 1918 and powerful Henry Cabot Lodge (R-Mass.) led the opposition on the Senate floor. In August, Wilson personally addressed the Senate to plea for woman suffrage as a wartime measure, recognizing the extraordinary contributions of the nation's women to the conflict. His message fell on too many deaf ears. On October 1, the vote of 62-34 was two shy of passage. After the 1918 fall elections, the lame-duck Senate again defeated the amendment, that time by only one vote.

The 1918 fall elections sent a Republican majority to both house of Congress, but the efforts of the suffragists did succeed in sending many new pro-suffrage representatives to Washington. Additionally, Michigan, South Dakota and Oklahoma joined the ranks of full suffrage states in 1918. Hope sprang eternal in the suffrage ranks, and it proved justified.

Carrie Catt was so sure of victory that she finalized her organization of the League of Women Voters before the vote was won. Usually blessed with foresight, Catt erred in her belief that the League would have a short life, just long enough to get women over the hump. Over eight decades later, the League is still providing the invaluable service of informing the electorate.

When the new Congress convened in 1919, the suffrage "map" showed pronounced regional differences. Of the fifteen states with full woman suffrage, all but two (New York and Michigan) were in the West.

1869 – Wyoming	1912 - Arizona
1870 - Utah	1914 - Nevada
1893 – Colorado	1914 - Montana
1896 – Idaho	1914 – New York
1910 – Washington	1918 - Michigan
1911 – California	1918 - South Dakota
1912 – Oregon	1918 - Oklahoma
1912 - Kansas	

A north-south string of eight mid-Atlantic and southern states had no suffrage at all. These were Pennsylvania, Maryland, West Virginia, Virginia, North Carolina, South Carolina, Georgia and Alabama. The remaining 25 states had partial suffrage ranging from local school boards to presidential. Most of the states with presidential suffrage were in the central and northern midlands, surrounding Illinois which pioneered that form of partial suffrage. States with other forms of partial suffrage were scattered mainly throughout the East and the south/southwestern parts of the country.

Put it all together and women in 28 of the 48 states could vote in the next presidential election, a fact that neither party could ignore.

The special session of the 65th Congress began on May 19, 1919. Republican James Mann of Illinois introduced in the House the woman suffrage bill on opening day and, expectedly, it passed 304-89 on May 21. The Senate debate began on June 2 and, with the entire suffrage movement holding it breath, passed the measure on June 4, 56-25. Tears, cheers, shocked disbelief, relief, exultation and prayerful thanksgiving swept thorough the land. Now it was up to Carrie Catt to ram it through three-quarters of the states' legislatures, thirty-six states in all. Would the struggle ever, ever end?

The Bitter End

Catt celebrated the congressional victory only briefly before embarking on her whirling dervish campaign for ratification. She telegrammed all the governors, beseeching them to call special sessions, and activated her two million members to lobby in each every state. She wanted action both quickly and simultaneously in many states so that opposition could not focus on one or two swing states at a time.

Illinois, Wisconsin and Michigan ratified immediately. Ratification quickly followed in Kansas, New York, Ohio, Pennsylvania, Massachusetts and Texas. Within the first four months, 17 of the necessary 36 states had ratified the Susan B. Anthony Amendment, and three had failed in Delaware, Georgia and Alabama.

Curiously western states, which had been the first to enfranchise women, were slow to act on ratification. So, Catt hopped on a train and toured the West for two months, expediting ratification efforts and simultaneously plugging her new League of Women Voters. During fall and early winter, 14 more states ratified, but Mississippi, South Dakota and Virginia voted the amendment down.

In the spring, ratification succeeded in New Mexico, Oklahoma, West Virginia and Washington, bring the total to 35, one short of the necessary number for ratification. The euphoria in the suffrage ranks began yielding to tension. None of the remaining states was a sure bet to ratify and some unquestionably would not. The most likely state was Tennessee, and pro and con activists from all over the country descended on Nashville to stage their version of the Gunfight at the O.K. Corral. It was precisely what Catt had hoped to avoid with a swift, early victory.

106

After the Tennessee Senate voted for ratification on August 13, 1920, desperate antis pulled out all the stops to influence the House vote. Catt wrote (Van Voris, p. 159):

> We now have 35.5 states .... With all the political pressure, it ought to be easy, but the opposition of every sort is here fighting with no scruple desperately. Women (including some former supporters who had turned against her) are here appealing to Negro phobia and every other cave man's prejudice. Men, lots of them, are here. What do they represent? God only knows. We believe they are buying votes. We have a poll of the House showing victory but they are trying to keep them at home, to break a quorum and God only knows the outcome. We are terribly worried and so is the other side. I've been here a month. It is hot, muggy nasty, and this last battle is desperate. We are low in our minds -- even if we win we who have been here will never remember it with anything but a shudder.

Catt added later (Van Voris, p. 160)

> Never in the history of politics had there been such a force for evil, such a nefarious lobby as labored to block the advance of suffrage in Nashville, Tenn. In the short time I spent in Tennessee's capital, I have been called more names, been more maligned, more lied about than in the thirty previous years I worked for suffrage. I was flooded with anonymous letters, vulgar, ignorant, insane. Strange men and groups of men sprang up, men we had never met before in battle. We were told this is the railroad lobby, this is the steel lobby, these are the lobbyists from the Manufacturers' Association,

**these come from the aluminum interests, this is
the remnant of the old whiskey ring. Even
tricksters from the United States Revenue
Service were there, operating against us, until
the President of these great States called them
off. They appropriated our telegrams, tapped
our telephones, listened outside our windows and
transoms. They attacked our private and public
lives.**

The blistering southern heat matched the intensity of the
debate in the House. One legislator had himself carried in
from his hospital bed so that he could vote for ratification.
Another supporter jumped off a train he was taking to see
his dying baby in order to vote yes. When the dust finally
settled, the vote was tied at 48, an apparent defeat for the
suffragists by one vote.

But not yet. Enter Harry Burns, a 24-year old
representative from Tennessee. He switched his vote to yes,
apparently making suffrage the law of the land.

But not yet. Burns was accused of being bribed, to
which he replied that he was keeping a pledge to his
mother. Then Speaker Walker, an anti, moved to
reconsider, which would give him three days to shake loose
one of the 49 favorables. When none wavered, 36 anti
legislators snuck out of town under cover of night, trying to
reduce the number of legislators present to less than a
quorum. When that failed, the opposition filed an
injunction, which Chief Justice Lansden immediately
rejected. Governor Roberts mailed the certificate of
ratification on August 24. U.S. Secretary of State
Bainbridge Colby received it on August 26 and declared
the Nineteenth Amendment to the Constitution ratified.

Finally it was over. At long last. At long, long, long last!
A 72-year struggle over two generations involving millions

of supporters was wondrously over. American women could finally vote. All of them. Everywhere. Weatherford concludes her 1998 book as follows.

> **Carrie Chapman Catt summed it up. Since the 1848 Seneca Falls call for the vote, she counted: 480 campaigns in state legislatures; 56 statewide referenda to male voters; 47 attempts to add suffrage planks during revisions of state constitutions; 277 campaigns at state party conventions and 30 at national conventions; and 19 biannual campaigns in 19 different Congresses. Literally thousands of times, men cast their votes on whether or not women should vote. Literally millions of women and men (dedicated themselves to) the cause and went to their graves with freedom unwon. No peaceful political change ever has required so much from so many for so long. None but a mighty army could have won.**

At peace at last were the spirits of Lucretia Mott, Elizabeth Cady Stanton, Lucy Stone, Susan B. Anthony, Sojourner Truth, Julia Ward Howe and the masses of less visible supporters. They planted the seeds in rocky soil that Carrie Catt, Alice Paul and their legions brought to fruit. Their names deserve to be as familiar as any in our history.

But they aren't. Instead, their monument is a simple, uncluttered, heroic combination of 28 words among the amendments to our nation's Constitution. Here is what they devoted their lives to.

> **The right of citizens of the United States to vote shall not be denied or abridged by the United States or by any States on account of sex.**
> Nineteenth Amendment,
> U.S. Constitution, 1920

Appendix I - State-by-State Progress in Full and Presidential Woman Suffrage

1869 - Wyoming Territory -- full suffrage
(statehood in 1890)
1870 - Utah Territory -- full suffrage
(statehood in 1896)
1893 - Colorado -- full suffrage
1896 - Idaho -- full suffrage
1910 - Washington -- full suffrage
1911 - California -- full suffrage
1912 - Oregon -- full suffrage
1912 - Kansas -- full suffrage
1912 - Arizona -- full suffrage
1913 - Illinois -- presidential suffrage
1914 - Montana -- full suffrage
1914 - Nevada -- full suffrage
1917 - North Dakota -- presidential suffrage
1917 - Nebraska -- presidential suffrage
1917 - Rhode Island -- presidential suffrage
1917 - New York -- full suffrage
1918 - Michigan -- full suffrage after presidential in 1917
1918 - South Dakota -- full suffrage
1918 - Oklahoma -- full suffrage
1919 - Indiana -- presidential suffrage
1919 - Maine -- presidential suffrage
1919 - Missouri -- presidential suffrage
1919 - Iowa -- presidential suffrage
1919 - Minnesota -- presidential suffrage
1919 - Ohio -- presidential suffrage
1919 - Wisconsin -- presidential suffrage
1919 - Tennessee -- presidential suffrage
1920 - Kentucky -- presidential suffrage

1920 - Nineteenth Amendment to the Constitution

1917 - Arkansas passed suffrage for primaries
1918 - Texas passed suffrage for primaries

Appendix II - The 1848 Seneca Falls Women's Rights Convention

Declaration of Sentiments

When, in the course of human events, it becomes necessary for one portion of the family of man to assume among the people of the earth a position different from that which they have hitherto occupied, but one to which the laws of nature and of nature's God entitle them, a decent respect to the opinions of mankind requires that they should declare the causes that impel them to such a course.

We hold these truths to be self-evident: that all men and women are created equal; that they are endowed by their Creator with certain inalienable rights; that among these are life, liberty, and the pursuit of happiness; that to secure these rights governments are instituted, deriving their just powers from the consent of the governed. Whenever any form of government becomes destructive of these ends, it is the right of those who suffer from it to refuse allegiance to it, and to insist upon the institution of a new government, laying its foundation on such principles, and organizing its powers in such form, as to them shall seem most likely to effect their safety and happiness. Prudence, indeed, will dictate that governments long established should not be changed for light and transient causes; and accordingly all experience hath shown that mankind are more disposed to suffer, while evils are sufferable, than to right themselves by abolishing the forms to which they are accustomed. But when a long train of abuses and usurpations, pursuing invariably the same object, evinces a design to reduce them under absolute despotism, it is their duty to throw off such government, and to provide new guards for their future security. Such has been the patient sufferance of the women under this government, and such is now the necessity which constrains them to demand the equal station to which they are entitled. The history of man is a history of repeated injuries and usurpations on the part of man toward woman, having in direct object the establishment of an absolute tyranny over her. To prove this, let the facts be submitted to a candid world.

He has never permitted her to exercise her right to the elective franchise.

He has compelled her to submit to laws, in the formation of which she had no vote.

He has withheld from her rights which are given to the most ignorant and degraded men -- both natives and foreigners.

Having deprived her of this first right of a citizen, the elective franchise, leaving her without representation in the halls of legislation, he has oppressed her on all sides.

He has made her, if married, in the eye of the law, civilly dead. He has taken from her all right in property, even to the wages she earns.

He has made her, morally, an irresponsible being, as she can commit many crimes with impunity, provided they be done in the presence of her husband.

In the covenant of marriage, she is compelled to promise obedience to her husband, he becoming, to all intents and purposes, her master -- the law giving him the power to deprive her of her liberty, and to administer chastisement.

He has so framed the laws of divorce, as to what shall be the proper causes, and in the case of separation, to whom the guardianship of the children shall be given, as to be wholly regardless of the happiness of women -- the law, in all cases, going upon a false supposition of the supremacy of man, and giving all power into his hands.

After depriving her of all rights as a married woman, if single, and the owner of property, he has taxed her to support a government which recognizes her only when her property can be made profitable to it.

He has monopolized nearly all the profitable employments. He closes against her all the avenues to wealth and distinction which he considers most honorable to himself. As a teacher of theology, medicine, or law, she is not known.

He has denied her the facilities for obtaining a thorough education, all colleges being closed against her.

He allows her in Church, as well as State, but a subordinate position, claiming Apostolic authority for her exclusion from the ministry, and, with some exceptions, from any public participation in the affairs of the Church.

He has created a false sentiment by giving to the world a different code of morals for men and women, by which more delinquencies which exclude women from society, are not only tolerated, but deemed of little account in man.

112

He has usurped the prerogative of Jehovah himself, claiming it as his right to assign for her a sphere of action, when that belongs to her conscience and to her God.

He has endeavored, in every way that he could, to destroy her confidence in her own powers, to lessen her self-respect and to make her willing to lead a dependent and abject life.

Now, in view of this disfranchisement of one-half the people of this country, their social and religious degradation -- in view of the unjust laws above mentioned, and because women do feel themselves aggrieved, oppressed, and fraudulently deprived of their most sacred rights, we insist that they have immediate admission to all the rights and privileges which belong to them as citizens of the United States.

In entering upon the great work before us, we anticipate no small amount of misconception, misrepresentation, and ridicule; but we will use every instrumentality within our power to effect our object. We shall employ agents, circulate tracts, petition the State and National legislatures, and endeavor to enlist the pulpit and the press in our behalf. We hope this Convention will be followed by a series of Conventions embracing every part of the country.

Resolutions

WHEREAS, The great precept of nature is conceded to be, that "man shall pursue his true and substantial happiness." Blackstone in his Commentaries remarks, that this law of Nature being coeval with mankind, and dictated by God ·himself, is of course superior in obligation to any other. It is binding all over the globe, in all countries and at all times; no human laws are of validity if contrary to this, and such of them as are valid, derive all their force, and all their validity, and all their authority, mediately and immediately, from this original; therefore,

Resolved, That such laws as conflict, in any way with the true and substantial happiness of woman, are contrary to the great precept of nature and of no validity, for this is "superior in obligation to any other."

Resolved, That all laws which prevent woman from occupying such a station in society as her conscience shall dictate, or which place her in a position inferior to that of man, are contrary to the great precept of nature, and therefore of no force or authority.

Resolved, That woman is man's equal -- was intended to be so by the Creator, and the highest good of the race demands that she should be regarded as such.

Resolved, That the women of this country ought to be enlightened in regard to the laws under which they live, that they may no longer publish their degradation by declaring themselves satisfied with their present position, nor their ignorance, by asserting that they have all the rights they want.

Resolved, That inasmuch as man, while claiming for himself intellectual superiority, does accord to woman moral superiority, it is pre-eminently his duty to encourage her to speak and teach, as she has an opportunity, in all religious assemblies.

Resolved, That the same amount of virtue, delicacy, and refinement of behavior that is required of woman in the social state, should also be required of man, and the same transgressions should be visited with equal severity on both man and woman.

Resolved, That the objection of indelicacy and impropriety, which is so often brought against woman when she addresses a public audience, comes with a very ill-grace from those who encourage, by their attendance, her appearance on the stage, in the concert, or in feats of the circus.

Resolved, That woman has too long rested satisfied in the circumscribed limits which corrupt customs and a perverted application of the Scriptures have marked out for her, and that it is time she should move in the enlarged sphere which her great Creator has assigned her.

Resolved, That it is the duty of the women of this country to secure to themselves their sacred right to the elective franchise.

Resolved, That the equality of human rights results necessarily from the fact of the identity of the race in capabilities and responsibilities.

Resolved, therefore, That, being invested by the Creator with the same capabilities, and the same consciousness of responsibility for their exercise, it is demonstrably the right and duty of woman, equally with man, to promote every righteous cause by every righteous means; and especially with regard to the great subjects of morals and religion, it is self-evidently her right to participate with her brother in teaching them, both in private and in public, by writing and by speaking, by any instrumentalities proper to be used, and in any assemblies proper to be held; and this being a self-evident truth growing out of the divinely implanted principles of human nature, any custom or authority adverse to it, whether modern or wearing the hoary sanction of antiquity, is to be regarded as a self-evident falsehood, and at war with mankind.

Resolved, That the speedy success of our cause depends upon the zealous and untiring efforts of both men and women, for the overthrow of the monopoly of the pulpit, and for the securing to woman an equal participation with men in the various trades, professions and commerce.

Guide to Further Reading

A. Internet

Most purchasers of my book learned of its existence through the Internet, so I have organized this section with their computer capabilities in mind.

There is so much free information on woman suffrage in the Internet that an interested person can, quite literally, download a foot of it in one day. Using any of the usual search engines, one needs only enter the names of the principal suffragettes to discover a bonanza of information. (Hint: except for Julia Ward Howe, omitting middle names and initials yields a larger number of "hits.") Additional keywords are women's rights, women's history and feminism. "Women's suffrage" yields more hits than "woman suffrage," by which the cause was first known.

A word or two of caution. The range of quality in the websites is greater than in more conventional publications, which requires the researcher to be critical and selective. Also, the relatively short length of most of the available works requires them to focus on small portions of the suffrage movement or just on one or two suffragettes. That requires readers to create an overall mosaic on their own.

Still, there's a gold mine of information in the Net and the reader should sample it. It's getting better all the time.

B. Books

The Internet also furnishes quite a few bibliographies which can direct the reader to conventional literature. These can be quite long for a very simple reason. The woman suffrage movement lasted so long and involved so many people in so many places that the accumulation of books in well over 100 years is staggering. Given this, the books I have cited in my text are only intended to ease the reader into four broad topics:

1. the broad context of women's history;
2. comprehensive coverage of the woman suffrage movement from beginning to end;
3. partial coverage of the movement;
4. related issues.

B1. The context of woman suffrage. The women's suffrage movement is only one sub-topic in the general context of women's history, which itself is a sub-topic within history in general. Understanding these broader contexts is more than a little helpful in understanding the agonies and the ecstasies of the suffrage movement. In this regard, I have found one particular softbound book delightfully insightful into women's history in the U.S., highly readable, affordable and still in print. It is:

Hymowitz, Carol and Michaele Weissman. **A History of Women in America.** New York: Bantam Books, 1978.

B2. Coverage from beginning to end. Few books even pretend to provide a comprehensive discussion of the entire suffrage movement from beginning to end. (I reduced my analysis to the major suffragette leaders to cover the movement from beginning to end in readable length.) There is a recent book that provides much more detail than my book and still remains quite readable. I highly recommend:

Weatherford, Doris. **A History of the American Suffragist Movement.** Santa Barbara, CA: ABC-CLIO, Inc., 1998.

The most detailed account of the woman suffrage movement from beginning to end is found in the six-volume, 6,000 page **History of Woman Suffrage.** Volume 1 was printed in 1881 and volume 6 in 1922. The whole series was reprinted in1969 by Arno and the New York Times and is most likely what you will find on inter-library loan. It's something of a career to read the whole thing, but it's also the best single source for the flavor of the suffrage movement as experienced by its leaders and as seen by its contemporaries. Volumes 1-3 were edited by Elizabeth Cady Stanton, Susan B. Anthony and Matilda Joslyn Gage; volume 4 by Anthony and Ida Husted Harper (1902); volumes 5 and 6 by Harper. It's massive, but also contains reams of primary source material not available elsewhere.

B3. Partial coverage of the woman suffrage movement. This is the bulk of the book literature that typically confines itself to one or two leaders, one period of time, a particular geographic region, a narrow dimension of the subject (e.g., the role of politics in women's rights) or specialized content (e.g., primary source documents).

I refer in my Preface to the 3.5 hour, two-video work of Ken Burnes and Paul Burns that features the half-century working relationship between Elizabeth Cady Stanton and Susan B. Anthony. Entitled **Not for Ourselves Alone,** the companion book to this 1999 video (the same title), and the video itself, may be ordered from the Public Broadcasting System (call your local station). Excellent work

Biographies, autobiographies and diaries abound and, unlike Barnes and Burns, usually focus on one person. Most are quite good. I recommend starting with short website profiles, then proceeding to whatever books are available locally and expanding selectively from there. The books I've cited in my text are:

Hays, Elinor Rise. **Morning Star.** New York: Octagon Press, 1978. (Biography of Lucy Stone)

Stanton, Elizabeth Cady. **Eighty Years and More.** New York: Schocken Books, 1971. (Autobiography)

Van Voris, Jacqueline. **Carrie Chapman Catt.** New York: Feminist Press, 1987. (Biography of Catt)

The political dimension of the woman suffrage movement is featured in this highly readable book:

Catt, Carrie Chapman and Nettie Rogers Shuler. **Woman Suffrage and Politics.** New York: Charles Scribner's Sons, 1923.

A good selection of hard-to-find primary source material (letters, speeches, Congressional testimony, etc.) is packed into this short volume.

Scott, Anne F and Andrew M. Scott. **One Half the People.** New York: J.B. Lippincott Co., 1975.

B4. Related Issues. Literature is easy to find on related issues such as the abolition movement, the temperance movement, Jacksonian democracy, industrialization and urbanization. Two books were cited in my text on the religious dimension of the suffrage movement.

Rogers, Jack, "Reading the Bible and Reflections on History," in **Renewing the Vision,** ed. by Cynthia M. Campbell. Louisville, KY: Geneva Press, 2000.

Stanton, Elizabeth Cady. **The Woman's Bible.** Boston: Northeastern University Press, 1993. The excellent forward in this volume provides considerable insight into the development of Stanton's personal religious convictions.